Violin Success Series : 2

# Performing at YOUR BEST!

A MUSICIAN'S GUIDE to
SUCCESSFUL PERFORMANCES

# Books by Ruth Shilling

- Accessing Clear Guidance: Help and Answers Through Inspired Writing & Inner Knowing
- Clear & Free of Unwanted Thoughts & Emotions: 25 Effective Methods

*Violin Success Series*
- SUCCESS with the Violin & Life: Strategies, Techniques, and Tips for Learning Quickly and Doing Well, Vol.1
- Performing at Your Best: A Musician's Guide to Successful Performances, Vol. 2

*Through A Medium's Eyes Series*
*About Life, Love, Mediumship, and the Spirit World*
- Rev. B. Anne Gehman, Vol. 1 (also in LARGE PRINT)
- Carol Gasber, Vol. 2
- Neal Rzepkowski, M.D., Vol. 3

*Books about Egypt*
- The Tomb of Queen Nefertari: Egyptian Gods & Goddesses of the New Kingdom
- Pictures of Ancient Egyptian Gods & Goddesses: Edited Photos
- Egyptian Gods & Goddesses Notebooks with Blank Papyrus-Imprint Pages, Vol. 1-16. Isis, Sekhmet, Horus, Ra, Anubis, Osiris, & more
- SINAI: The Desert & Bedouins of South Sinai's Central Regions. Photos and text by Ruth Shilling.
- Time & Space in the Temples & Pyramids: Egypt Tour

*Adult Coloring Books*
- Marvelous Manifestation Mandalas, Vol. 1
- Magnetic Manifestation Mandalas, Vol. 2
- Miraculous Manifestation Mandalas, Vol. 3
- Angelic Manifestation Mandalas, Vol. 4

*Violin Success Series : 2*

# Performing at YOUR BEST!

## A MUSICIAN'S GUIDE to SUCCESSFUL PERFORMANCES

## RUTH SHILLING

All One World Books & Media

Performing at Your Best: A Musician's Guide to Successful Performances. *Violin Success Series, Book 2.*

Print book ISBN: 978-0-9971991-8-5

eBook ISBN: 978-0-9971991-7-8

Text, interior illustrations, and cover design: Ruth Shilling

Published by All One World Books & Media

all1world.com

Copyright © 2020 by Ruth Shilling

All rights reserved.

Some of the material in this book is also included in Book 1 of the *Violin Success Series – Success with the Violin and Life*, also authored by Ruth Shilling.

**Violin Success Series**: violinsuccess.com

Facebook.com/successviolin

Ruth Shilling: ruthshilling.com

Facebook.com/ruthshillingmm

# Table of Contents

Introduction .................................................................... ix

**CHAPTER ONE: Having a Clear "Sound Idea" ............. 1**
    SOUND IDEAS ........................................................................ 4
    CREATING YOUR "SOUND IDEA" ..................................... 6
    A CONCEPT of the WHOLE PIECE ...................................... 9
        *Story: Hearing the Brahms Requiem in a New Way* ...................... 9
    INSPIRED PLAYING ............................................................. 11

**CHAPTER TWO: Embody the Feeling ........................... 15**
    CREATING A "BODY FEELING IMAGE" ......................... 15
    ARRIVAL NOTES: Climax Notes, Big Shifts (string players), Cadences, and other Important Notes .................................. 20
    VISUALIZATION: Developing Your Own "Paganini Practice Technique," Imagining the Muscle Movements ................... 25
        *Story: The Paganini Practicing Technique* ................................. 25
        *Story: Winning at the Hurdles* .................................................. 26
    TRANSFORMING EVENTS ................................................. 32
    NEGATIVES ........................................................................... 33
        *Story: "This time I won't screw up."* ........................................ 33

**CHAPTER THREE: MAKING IT RELIABLE ................ 35**
    Preparing a Piece for Performance Will Go Through a Number of Phases: ............................................................... 37
    Step 3. REPETITION, MAKING IT MORE RELIABLE ....... 39

Step 4. GIVE IT TIME TO DIGEST ..................................................... 44

## CHAPTER FOUR:
## MAKING IT SOLID UNDER PRESSURE ....................... 45

Step 5. WAYS TO SOLIDIFY A PIECE ............................................. 47
*Story: Just Running the Bartok Concerto* ............................. 52
*Story: Iiiiiiizzzzzzzzzzz-zzzzz-zzzz!* ........................................ 55
Step 6. STAMINA – MAINTAINING FOCUS & ENDURANCE ... 59

## CHAPTER FIVE: WHEN MISTAKES HAPPEN ............ 63

Staying Focused and Keeping Going When Mistakes Happen ........ 63
*Story: Breaking a Habit* ............................................................ 65

## CHAPTER SIX: MEMORIZING YOUR MUSIC ............ 69

THREE MODALITIES FOR MEMORIZATION ...................... 70
GENERAL .................................................................................... 71
*Being Able to Start Anywhere in the Piece* .......................... 71
1. AUDITORY MEMORY ......................................................... 72
*Story: A Break in Memory When a Piece was Memorized Using Only Auditory Memory* ............................................... 72
2. VISUAL MEMORY ................................................................ 80
3. MUSCLE MEMORY ............................................................... 85
4. USING ASSOCIATION to AID YOUR MEMORY ............. 91

## CHAPTER SEVEN: PERFORMANCE NERVES ........... 93

OVERALL APPROACH, Dealing with Nerves ......................... 94
*Story: Fire, fire!* ........................................................................ 99
*Story: A French Menu* ............................................................ 99
HANDLING THE EXTRA ENERGY ....................................... 101
MAKE A RECORDING – SOUND, VIDEO ............................ 105

PLAYING IN FRONT OF A PRACTICE AUDIENCE ............... 106
## CHAPTER EIGHT: STAGE FRIGHT ................ 111
STAGE FRIGHT ................................................................. 111
THE PRIMAL FEAR: CROWD ATTACK, DEVASTATING JUDGEMENT/CRITICISM ................................................ 117
WHO IS YOUR AUDIENCE? ........................................... 121
    *Story #1, String Quartet* ............................................... 122
    *Story #2, Beethoven Septet* ......................................... 122
    *Story #3, Clarinetist* ..................................................... 124
REALITY CHECK, THE AUDIENCE ............................... 125
    *Story: The Winning Basketball Coach* ....................... 134
DEALING WITH THE FEAR ITSELF ............................... 135
STEP BY STEP: OVERCOMING FEAR ............................ 138
    *Story: Scared to Dive* ................................................... 138
OTHER WAYS TO DEAL WITH FEAR ........................... 145
    *Story: Brahms Quintet* ................................................ 146
KNOW THAT FEAR DOES NOT NEED TO STOP YOU, Having Courage ................................................................ 148
    *Story: Playing Through Her Fear* ............................... 148
## CHAPTER NINE: WHERE WILL YOU PERFORM? .. 151
AUDITIONING .................................................................. 153
    *Story: His Personality Disqualified Him* .................. 157
CONCERTS & RECITALS *Make It Your Gift to The Audience* ..... 159
PERFORMING IS A PACKAGE: *It is Not Just Playing the Music* .160
## CHAPTER TEN: THE BASICS ............................. 165
## About the Author ................................................. 172

## BONUS CHAPTER:
## SUCCESS with the VIOLIN and LIFE .......................... 175

### CHAPTER ONE: Practice Being Successful ....................................... 175

Story: Success Breeds Success........................................................ 176

### REPEATEDLY DOING SOMETHING WELL
### The Best Use of Your Practice Time ................................................. 181

## Building from Success to Success in Life ...................... 184

Story: One Success Builds to Greater Successes............................ 184

Story: "I can play every note in every piece of music."................. 185

# Introduction

## "I Played It Better at Home"

Every music teacher has heard (hundreds of times for many of us) a bewildered student say in a lesson, "But I played it better at home." One teacher I know even has those words on a plaque hanging in her studio.

Why don't we always perform at our best? And how can we make it more likely that when we are in front of an audience, we *will* play, if not at our *all-time best*, at least in a way that we can feel good about it and even proud of?

Athletes work to improve their skills with the hope that on the day of the competition they will equal their best time or score and even surpass it. Likewise, as musicians, there are those performances when we surpass ourselves, but most of the time, we will be happy if our performances just go as well as we played it at home or in rehearsal.

Those of us who have performed under a wide range of conditions and venues have learned that we usually lose a percentage of what we *could* do when we are performing. Less-experienced performers may lose 70% of their skill level when in front of an audience. As people grow more accustomed to performing and do it more frequently, they may only lose 10%. Seasoned musicians who perform multiple times a week may be performing at 100% of their skill level.

There are a few reasons we don't always perform at our best. First of all, we also don't always play our best when we are practicing at home either. If you have played a piece 100 times at home, and 80 of those times you made some mistakes, there is only a 20% chance that you will play it without mistakes the 101$^{st}$ time you play it, either at home or in front of others.

If you don't often play in front of an audience, and get a bit nervous, you will likely lose at least 50% of your skill level. Now your chance of playing that piece without mistakes in front of an audience is only 10%!

There are a number of different components that contribute to performing at our best. This book covers:

1. How to **solidify your own skill level** with a piece of music. This includes having a clear *sound idea* – a clear notion of how you want it to sound and how it feels to play it that way – and being able to play it consistently at that skill level. Can you play it correctly 100 times out of 100 or 10 times out of 10 or just sometimes yes, sometimes no?

2. There is a section on **memorization**. How can you play it consistently well, if you don't remember how it goes?

3. **Nerves**. Most of us have to deal with this in one way or another. This topic has been divided into two chapters. The first deals with the normal sort of nervousness that most musicians have both before and during their performances.

The next chapter talks about all-out **stage fright** – why it is normal to have that fear ("fear of public speaking" is said to be even more prevalent than "fear of death") and ways you can deal with that. Hopefully that chapter will give you a widened perspective about stage fright and some tools to help you move past it into performances you feel good about.

The final chapter is a quick review to bring it all together in a short, neat package for you. There is also a bonus chapter from the ***Success with the Violin and Life*** book at the end. Some of the material in this book is included in that book but in a much shorter form. That book has 20 chapters, so includes many other topics.

I hope you enjoy it and find it fruitful.

*To your successful performances!*

*Ruth Shilling*

## CHAPTER ONE

# Having a Clear "Sound Idea"

### What Are You Playing?

*The clearer we are about
what we want it to sound like,
the easier it will be to play it that way.*

SOUND IDEAS
- How Do I Want It to Sound? How Does It Go?
CREATING YOUR "SOUND IDEA"
A CONCEPT of the WHOLE PIECE
INSPIRED PLAYING
YOUR PERSONAL "SOUND IDEA" OF THE PIECE

When you first get out of bed in the morning, you probably make your way to the kitchen or bathroom. If you are in reasonably good health, it is unlikely that you question whether your feet and legs will carry you where you want to go. Why?

**You have confidence:**

- in your ability to walk upright
- in your ability to balance your weight on your feet
- that your feet and legs will carry you
- in your ability to gauge the distance and know the route to where you are going – where to stop, turn, etc.
- that no one is going to judge, criticize or evaluate you on your walking-to-the-kitchen abilities
- that your kitchen or bathroom still exist and have not disappeared during the night

All of these things give you the confidence to step out of bed without fear and walk to your first destination.

**If you had that same easy confidence when walking out on stage to perform, wouldn't that feel good?**

Staying with the getting-up-in-the-morning example, what about if you had an injury to one of your legs or for some reason you needed a walker to get around? If your walker was not there and you needed to get to the bathroom, this could be pretty anxiety-producing. Why? Because you did not feel capable. You did not have the confidence in your ability to walk without assistance.

So, in order to perform the act of walking in the morning, you need to have **confidence in your ability** to walk.

Likewise, **the first component in creating a successful performance is to have the confidence in your ability to play your piece of music.** If you are worried about a particularly difficult passage, how can you feel that sureness and confidence to play your best? So solidifying your expertise is of the utmost importance. More about that in Chapter 3.

But first, how is it that your body knows how to roll out of bed, put your feet on the floor, stand up, and walk? What makes all that possible?

Over time, the patterns of how to do that have been imprinted repeatedly and embedded in your subconscious. The language of that part of us is symbolic. The pattern that is *the set of commands to the mind and body* could be called the *idea* of performing that action.

This *idea* is a multi-facetted "package" of all that goes into executing that action (in this case, getting out of bed and walking). There are many different muscle groups and body systems that need to work well together to create that action – the *idea* that we call "getting up in the morning."

## SOUND IDEAS

For a musical performance, we have **sound ideas** which guide both our bodies and minds in the execution of the musical piece we are playing. The clearer this *sound idea* is, the more successful the actions will be which result from it.

**The best is when the SOUND IDEA includes
the actual sound of the music in our minds
and a reliable *body feeling image*.**

**The *body feeling image* is
the physical-body-memory "package" –
the imprint of what it feels like
when we are playing it easily and correctly.**

If a musician is not clear on both the actual *sound they are intending*, and the *body feeling image* of doing it, a good, satisfying performance is unlikely.

This chapter will include strategies on creating a clear version of how you want it to sound. Chapter 2 will go into training the *body feeling image*. Chapter 3 and 4 have strategies for solidifying your skill in playing your piece of music. Later chapters will talk about dealing with performance anxiety and other topics.

## How Do I Want It to Sound?  How Does It Go?

One musician described his **sound ideas** as being like a little man playing in his head and he is trying his best to play it just that way. Another described it as a recording playing in her head which she tries to match as she plays.

Both these musicians are quite clear about the sounds they are striving for. Less advanced players often are not so sure. Instead, they may play the notes that are written as best they can, and then find out what it sounds like – thus formulating their idea of the piece that way.

Unfortunately, what can happen is that as they are learning the piece, they play out of tune or with the wrong rhythms (or both!). This becomes their personal version of the piece. If they then want to play it correctly, they have to *unlearn* their own personal version (which is harder than it was to learn it in the first place) and replace it with the correct rhythms and good intonation.

Dr. Shinichi Suzuki, the founder of the *Suzuki Violin Method* (which was later also applied to other instruments) bypassed this mistake by having the students listen to the pieces many, many times before the students began to play them. He called this the "mother tongue method."

By listening repeatedly to the correct versions of the pieces, the students did not fall into the trap of creating their own versions (with incorrect rhythms). Their left-hand intonation was often still limited by their present skill levels, but at least (hopefully), they had an idea how it should sound!

One of my teachers joked that no one can play Mozart in tune because when we first learned it, we were students. Later, when we play it as mature musicians, we revert back to our previous mistakes and weaknesses in performing it. Our old *sound idea*, with our original less-than-precise intonation, dictates how we play it, even though we now have the ability to do a much better job.

# CREATING YOUR "SOUND IDEA"

### === STRATEGY ===

### 1. Figure out the rhythms.

Before playing a new piece, take some time to figure out the beats and subdivisions for any complicated rhythms. This is especially true in slow movements that have 32nd and 64th notes interspersed with long notes.

## 2. Tap & sing the rhythms.

Be sure that you can tap and sing all the rhythms in your piece correctly while using a metronome. Pay extra attention to any complex rhythms that are not what you would expect them to be.

## 3. Subdivisions on long notes.

On long notes, make a mental imprint of what the subdivisions should be. For a whole note, say out loud (and later think) 4 sets of 16th notes. You may want to use a 4-syllable word, like "pepperoni."

## 4. Subdivide before playing 16ths.

If you have a series of rests and will play 16th notes when you come in, in your mind begin counting the 16th note subdivisions in the preceding beats before you play.

## 5. Rests.

During the rests, count out loud. If possible, sing what someone else is playing during your rest while tapping the beats at the same time.

## 6. Sing the intervals.

Check that you can sing all the intervals that you will play. Put it into a range that suits your voice.

## 7. Know the sound of the next note.

You need to know what the next note will sound like while you are still playing the preceding note. You can train this by singing the next note out loud while still playing the previous note. It can be easier to do this with the piano (instead of singing while playing other instruments), but figure out the best way that works for you.

## 8. Musical phrasing.

To improve your musical phrasing, sing each phrase in a faster tempo. Once you can sing it easily in a very fast tempo, the whole phrase will make more sense to you. You will get the big picture of how it is shaped, where it is going, and the overarching concept that is being expressed.

Next, slow it down incrementally so that you hear how the details begin to fit into the whole phrase as it gets slower.

It is something like watching a video of an athlete doing a particular move and then seeing it in super slow motion. Create phrases that have that same smooth and unwavering path to their destination.

# A CONCEPT of the WHOLE PIECE

At first, we may only be able to know what the next few notes will be. Then we move on to holding a whole phrase in our minds, then larger and larger sections.

## *Story:*
## *Hearing the Brahms Requiem in a New Way*

When I was a music student in college, we performed the Brahms Requiem. I played in the orchestra for the performance, but also learned the alto part because one of the requirements for all music majors was to sing in the chorus. We worked on the Requiem for most of the semester, so with all those rehearsals, I not only knew my own parts well, but everyone else's, too. By the end of the semester, I felt I knew that piece inside and out.

Later when I studied in Berlin, Germany, I went to a performance of the Brahms Requiem with Herbert von Karajan conducting the Berlin Philharmonic Orchestra. During that performance, I experienced the Requiem in a new way.

I hadn't realized it, but in my mind the individual movements were quite separate. For me it had been as though each movement was a piece unto itself and they were just played one after the other.

As Karajan conducted, I experienced the whole Requiem as one large piece. All the movements still had their own individual integrity and beauty, but now I heard how each belonged within the larger whole, each one adding to it and at the same time fitting within it.

It was magnificent.

I also knew that Karajan had been holding the entire Requiem in his mind as he made his first down beat. Every note had its place in his all-encompassing vision of what that performance was to be.

Thank you to a legendary musician for giving me that profound experience and teaching me something about our human potential.

*The more advanced a musician becomes,
the more music
he can hold in his mind at once.*

===

# INSPIRED PLAYING

One of my friends is fond of saying, "The voice does not lie." What she means by that is that the quality of a person's voice gives away what it is they are truly feeling, the state they are really in. A person may say that everything is just fine, but the heavy sorrow in her voice will give her away.

Likewise, when we are playing music, we are expressing. Your instrument is your voice. If you feel that the piece you are playing is boring, it will sound that way. If you are actually angry about something or feeling competitive, your playing will sound that way, too.

So, to play in an inspired way, we need to embody the state of being inspired. If the piece calls for playing a passage with warmth or tenderness, we won't be able to convey that if we are focusing on how angry we are about something.

How can we embody the states we want to convey with the music? A person's inner communication vocabulary is unique to each one of us.

However, here are some ideas.

=== STRATEGIES ===

## Embodying the State You Want the Music to Convey

### • Putting Words to It

Make the melody into a song that is giving people a message or telling them a story.

### • Story Line

Let each phrase tell more about a story as it unfolds throughout the piece.

### • Characterizations

Choose a character from a book, movie or story, or make up one of your own. Imagine that character as you play. Hear them singing what you are playing or how their voice might sound.

*Examples: People, animals, cartoons, puppets.*

### • Visual Images

Picture scenes or visual impressions that bring up certain feelings or emotions for you.

*Example: A ray of sunlight coming through the clouds in a sky that is still partially dark from a storm.*

- **Body Sensations**

Rocking, swaying, reaching, throwing, dancing, crouching, pushing, stroking something soft, breezes, cold, hot…

*Example: Swaying on a porch swing on a warm summer night with a light breeze and the smell of jasmine in the air.*

- **Memories**

Go into your past memories and see if the character of the music reminds you of something from your life experiences.

- **Sound only, without tangible associations**

Be in the flow of the pure sound as an experience that goes beyond physical life experiences.

- **Sound as a vehicle that carries you**

In the same way that an airplane takes you to a new place or a river carries you to a different destination, sound can carry us to other realms and experiences. Ride the sound.

## YOUR PERSONAL SOUND IDEA OF THE PIECE

Listening to multiple performers play the piece you are working on can be helpful, as it can widen the possibilities you may have thought of yourself. It may also inspire you to push past some of your own technical limitations.

However, in the end, each one of us will put our personal imprint on a musical piece through our own interpretation. That is part of the magic of being a musician; we get to do that. We are both the lover and the creator.

# CHAPTER TWO

# Embody the Feeling

CREATING A "BODY FEELING IMAGE"
GOAL TEMPO, Fast Notes
ARRIVAL NOTES: Climax Notes, Big Shifts for string players,
  Cadences, and Other Important Notes
VISUALIZATION: Developing Your Own "Paganini
  Practice Technique"

## CREATING A "BODY FEELING IMAGE"

### Goal: Confidence, Solidity and Ease

At some point, you have probably lived in a house with some stairs. At first you needed to look at the stairs to see how steep they were. After going up and down them multiple times, you could climb those stairs while carrying something that blocked your ability to see them. Because you now had a *body feeling image* of how to navigate those stairs, you were still able to do it.

What a pleasure it is when you can play a piece of music with that same ease and confidence. In the same way that we hear in our mind what we want the music to sound like, when we are well prepared to play a piece, there is also a *body feeling image* in our memory of what it FEELS like to play it well. The clearer this is, the better.

A soloist who stands and waits while the orchestra or pianist plays an introduction needs to have a clear *body feeling image* of what it will feel like when she plays her first note. It cannot be a chancy surprise. She needs to know what the sound is, but also the physical feeling of playing that first note.

If we invest a bit in clarifying for ourselves the *body feeling images* that make things work, **we can speed up the time it takes to learn new music.** In a way, it is like learning different dance steps. Someone describes what to do first, then you repeat it a number of times, and eventually it gets easy and smooth.

With a new piece of music, it isn't someone else teaching us the steps, we are the ones teaching ourselves by **noticing what we are doing and how we can best do it.** One way to help the process along is to question ourselves when something works with **"How did that just feel?"**

*EXAMPLE: There is a wave-form motion I find myself doing with the bow when I do the bariolage (alternating between two strings). It works best when my focus is on the middle of that wave. Like there is an even line and the wave goes above and below it.*

If possible, notice the sensations in your fingers, arms, mouth (whatever you use to play or sing) and "paint a picture" for yourself of all the muscle movements that are needed working together as a whole.

## GOAL TEMPO, Fast Notes

It is helpful to think about how it will feel when you play something at your goal tempo. It can also help if you remember some other piece that has some similarities to the new piece and how you felt when you were playing that piece.

*Example: When I played that fast piece with all the 16$^{th}$ notes, I got to the point where my body was moving quickly but there wasn't any tension. It felt like dancing. I want to get that same feeling for the fast passage in this new piece.*

### LESS EFFORT => SPEED

**The less effort needed, the faster we can play.
Fast passages need to be played with minimal effort.**

When a car is traveling in first gear, it has more power to climb hills or get the car moving from a standstill. Using all that power, however, also means that the car cannot travel very fast in first gear. If the car is in fourth or fifth gear it does not have as much power, but it can propel the car at much faster speeds.

Likewise, when we want to play a long string of fast notes, we need to be able to execute those notes with a minimum amount of effort (power). The less effort we need to play the notes, the faster we will be able to play them.

=== STRATEGY ===

## Speeding Up a String of Fast Notes

When you are practicing a passage with the goal of being able to play it faster, it helps to practice it **in a slow tempo with precision while using the least amount of effort.** As you need less and less effort to play it, you will be able to easily increase it to a faster tempo.

A good strategy is to play it repeatedly at an easy speed being careful that you stay *exactly* with the metronome. Don't let it be approximate. It should line up precisely with the clicks of the metronome.

As you play, monitor how your muscles are working, and if they fit the *body feeling image* you will need to play the notes at the goal tempo for your performance.

## Your goal is to play with Precision, Reliability, and Ease

**Record yourself** playing the piece or passage. It is important that the clicks of the metronome also be clearly heard on the recording. When you listen to the recording, check that every note is lining up with those clicks.

Easily and gracefully work it up to a faster speed. As you do that, monitor that you are remaining in good control of your muscles while not creating tension.

As you are monitoring yourself, if you notice yourself tensing up in any way, slow it back down. Play it multiple times at the slower tempo to reinforce the skill of playing it perfectly without excessive effort. Use the least amount of effort needed to play the notes at exactly the right time.

**Experiment with how lightly you can put down your fingers and still have it work.**

Often people are pressing much more than is actually needed with their fingers. When a person practices lifting weights and their muscles develop, the impression is that the weights they started with are getting lighter.

The muscles that move your fingers on your instrument are like that, too. Over the years you will need less and less effort to play at the same speed.

There are many additional ways to internalize a series of notes. Every musician probably has their favorites.

Examples: dotted rhythms, short bits at a faster tempo that get chain-linked together, singing it faster… (see the *Success with the Violin and Life* book for additional suggestions).

When using any of these strategies, the same idea applies. For the best results, the notes should be played with the same **graceful precision** you will need when playing faster. **No tensing up or exerting lots of effort.**

## ARRIVAL NOTES: Climax Notes, Big Shifts (string players), Cadences, and other Important Notes.

The example below is for shifting to a note, so it will apply directly to string players. However, the concepts will suit any instrument as you follow through the steps. This strategy can be applied to any arrival note or other important note.

=== STRATEGY ===

# Playing Arrival Notes with Confidence and Accuracy

**1. Pitch. Play the arrival note only.**

Be sure that you can play the note you want to arrive on exactly in tune (use a tuner, if necessary) and with a good full rich tone.

**2. Dynamic & tone (bowing style).**

• Play the arrival note with the **same dynamic** (loud-soft) that you will play this note in the context of the piece. You want to feel pleased with how the note sounds. Does it fit with how you envision that note sounding in the context of your ideal *sound idea* of the piece?

• Use the **same articulation and tone quality (bowing style)** that you will want it to have in the context of the piece.

For string players: Notes played in the upper positions result in a shorter string length. This means you will need to play closer to the bridge to find the **Sounding Point** where the note resonates most freely. Playing closer to the bridge will mean more weight is needed on the string to produce a good tone. Also keep in mind the bow speed you will be using for this note. This will also affect the amount of weight, and hence how close to the bridge you need to play.

**BECOME THE OBSERVER.** When you hit it just right, notice how that feels. Notice how your body feels – fingers, arms, posture, all of it. Memorize that feeling by evaluating it and putting it into words or some other way of expressing it to yourself. **"This is how it feels when I get it just right."**

### 3. Rhythm, arrival note and following notes.

Beginning on the arrival note, play the arrival note and the following group of notes with the correct rhythm and in the tempo that it will occur in the piece. Does it match your *sound idea?*

### 4. Solidify this with repetition and satisfaction.

Starting on the arrival note, play the passage imbuing it with a feeling of satisfaction and sureness. Think, "Yes! Good," as you hit it just right.

*Note: This is like the target shooter hitting the bullseye. His pattern was: Success, Rejoice, Satisfaction. See his story in the Bonus Chapter at the end of this book.*

### 5. Play (only) the notes that are before the arrival note.

Make sure they are solid. Stop just before the arrival note.

### 6. Add two beats of rest before playing the arrival note.

Using the metronome, begin at a convenient place before the arrival note and play the passage until you get to the arrival note.

Stop before playing the arrival note and add two or more beats of rest before playing it. Use these two beats to move to the note and prepare yourself so that you can play it with ease and confidence **just the way you practiced it in Steps 1-4.**

If this feels hurried, choose the number of beats you need to feel comfortable and get it right.

**During the rests envision playing the arrival note before moving to it and playing it.**

- Hear it in your head.

- Know how it will feel in your fingers (and bow) and the rest of your body.

- Remember the good feeling of playing it.

- Once you have the whole thing in your mind, move to it and play. *"Yes! Good."*

**7. Make it only one beat of rest.**

Once you are solid and comfortable with the two beats of rest, make it only one beat of rest before the arrival note.

## 8. Sing the passage with the metronome.

This is to be sure that you can imagine how it will sound when you leave out the added rest. Singing it will help remind you of your *Sound Idea*.

## 9. Sing the preceding notes, then play on the arrival note.

Only begin to play on the arrival note, sing the preceding notes. Play it with the same confidence and good sound that you perfected in Steps 1-4.

## 10. Play that short passage as written.

Be sure that before you play the arrival note that you know just what you are about to do. Hear it in your mind, know the feeling in your body of doing it right, and envision your satisfying *sound idea*.

**When you feel that sweet success, ENJOY IT!**

# VISUALIZATION:
## Developing Your Own "Paganini Practice Technique," Imagining the Muscle Movements.

### Story: The Paganini Practicing Technique

There is a story of a man who thought he could discover the violinist Niccolo Paganini's magic by eavesdropping while Paganini prepared for a concert. What exactly was his practicing technique? The man was quite puzzled when he heard no sound at all. When Paganini was asked why he was not practicing, he replied that the way he practiced was to go over it all in his head.

If you can visualize exactly what and how you will play – fingering, bowing, breathing, sound – your ability to play a piece will soar!

===

Athletes are particularly aware of the value of visualization and are often able to easily measure the results. If it gives them a faster clock time, higher batting average, or lower number of strokes in golf, they can easily measure the effectiveness of working with visualization.

Visualization can be used for rehearsing their moves in their minds, for seeing their desired outcomes, and for holding a sustained laser-like focus. They can also use it to develop and employ powerful metaphors that expand them beyond their previous limitations, best scores or timings.

### Story: Winning at the Hurdles

I remember listening to an interview with an Olympic athlete who had won a hurdle event. He said that what was different about his technique was that his focus was on his time in the air instead of on the ground. In his mind, he was basically flying over the hurdles and touching down a bit in between each one. The strength of his flying image helped him to soar past the others and win each race.

===

# Create impressions on the Subconscious Powerhouse of Creativity

The subconscious mind plays a major role in creating what happens in our lives. Therefore, to be most effective, the subconscious mind needs to be incorporated into any strategy for creating a desired outcome.

People with a meditation practice can use those skills for going into a *relaxed-but-alert* state and imprinting their mind and body with a *sound idea*. This might be a *sound idea* they have previously created of themselves playing their piece in front of an audience, or it could be one where they are playing a certain passage successfully.

Two other ideal times to work with the subconscious mind are just before we sleep and as we are waking up.

> **The final thoughts before sleeping and
> the first thoughts upon waking are very potent.**

Here are some suggestions for utilizing those important times. The effects of doing these exercises are quite amazing and wonderful!

## In the Morning Upon Waking

### SHORT VERSION (Morning)

If you only have a short amount of time before starting your day, a one-sentence general statement of intent or affirmation may work best for you. It helps to write it down and keep it in a handy place. Your statement/affirmation could be about playing some part of your piece in a satisfactory way or doing well on an upcoming performance.

Declare your statement/affirmation **three times** either aloud or in your mind (aloud is better), then, as you begin going about your day think of at least a few times when you were able to play your instrument in an easy, confident way.

## It is important the statement has the following characteristics:

**1. Stated as though it has already occurred.**

*Example: "Boy, that felt good to play it at 138 for the quarter note. I felt like I was just cruising along!"*

*Example: "Wow! I did it! That concert went so well!"*

Do you want to have the experience of actually having achieved it, or do you want to be always hoping that in the future you will? This is why prayers will often end with, "It is done." If the prayer was, "I want it to happen in the future," that means, "I want to be in the state where it has not happened yet." In other words, I want to be in the state of *not having it*.

**2. Stated in the positive, no negative words** like *not, never, wasn't, etc.* The subconscious hears what nouns and verbs you use without taking into account any negating of those. See NEGATIVES below.

**3. Make it believable.** If you are telling yourself something that you know isn't true or is highly unlikely, it will often just be immediately deleted by the mind's BS detector.

Better, faster results come about by reinforcing the potentials which are believable to us. We can keep upgrading the statement/affirmation as we come closer to our ultimate goals.

## LONGER VERSION
**(Morning or as a Practice-time Break)**

If you have more time in the morning, you can work with visualizing yourself playing your piece. Hear it in your mind or sing it to yourself as you imagine which finger is playing each note and how it feels as you do that. Where and how will you breathe? String players should also imagine the bowing.

This is also a good way to **break up your practice time** into sections. You can be like Paganini and lie down and go through what you are working on in your head. Then go back to playing it again.

Our muscles get tired as we work on our music for long periods of time. When I spent 5-6 hours a day practicing and then had rehearsals in the evenings, I discovered that if I stopped before my muscles began to rebel, I could put in a lot more practice time in total.

I would set a timer for 50 minutes and make myself stop and take a break when it went off. If I continued to play without stopping at all for more than 75-90 minutes, my muscles would give out, and I would not be able to continue practicing.

**Start with something easy**

If you haven't worked with visualization before, it is recommended to **pick a small passage, or even simply playing a scale.** Hear it, feel it. It is a skill that is developed over time, so it's best to move into it in a way that you can have the pleasure of succeeding at it.

**Later**

A more advanced step is to **hear all the other parts that are playing** while you play your own part. Hear it, feel yourself playing it, and feel your emotions (including your satisfaction in playing it well).

# At Night Before Sleeping

As you review your day, try to remember how your practicing went or any rehearsals and concerts you played that day. Notice what went well and what did not. If possible, use this as a time to investigate rather than to get emotionally worked up about things that bothered you.

### 1. Events that Did Go Well – What You Want More Of

Acknowledging and appreciating the events that you feel pleased with and are grateful for will help bring more of those situations into your life. It might be just one small section of a piece or one thing that happened in rehearsal. Now that you realize how pleasant it was, you may find yourself paying more attention to the times things went well. This will actually set up a pattern where more experiences happen that please you.

## 2. Events that Did Not Go Well

When you find an event that was not what you would have wanted it to be, you can try the TRANSFORMING EVENTS strategy (below).

## 3. For the Future

Once the day has been reviewed – acknowledged, appreciated and cleaned up – you can also move into embedding projections for the future using your statement/affirmation (see Short Version – Morning above). If you are repeating that statement/affirmation as you drift off to sleep, it will have tremendous potency.

# TRANSFORMING EVENTS

### 1. Evaluate, find out
What about that event was not to your liking? What didn't you like about it?

### 2. What would have been better?
If you could do it over again, what would you do differently? How would you respond or act in a way that you now (lying in bed and thinking about it) would feel good? If you had been feeling powerful, highly competent, and skillful, what would you have done in that situation?

If it is difficult to find how you wish you had acted, or what you think would be the best way to handle something, think of someone you admire and ask yourself what that person would have done. It could be someone you know, a musician you admire, one of your teachers…

### 3. Rescript it & run the new version
Once you can think of a preferred scenario for the unpleasant event during your day, rescript it. Run the situation in your mind with the new preferred actions and outcomes.

This will affect future events that have similarities to it.

**Note that this is not about making a value judgment.** Saying, "I want to play it better," will not help. It is important to visualize *what it is you want it to be.*

# NEGATIVES

As stated above, the **Statement/Affirmation** should be in the positive. No use of words like no, not or don't. Unfortunately, the subconscious evidently does not understand negatives and just delivers whatever the literal meaning of a statement is without the negatives. "I will not mess up," becomes, "I will mess up."

### *Story: "This time I won't screw up."*

Someone sent me a card with a Gary Larson *Farside* cartoon on the front. The picture is a percussionist standing in the orchestra wearing his concert clothes. Above him, the words in the thought-callout say, "This time I won't screw up. I won't, I won't, I won't, I won't …" In one hand is a cymbal and the other hand is held as though it is holding the other cymbal, but… it is empty. The caption below reads, "Roger screws up."

===

I think every musician has had an experience like this at some point. The more we say, "I won't screw up," the more likely we are to do just that.

## CHAPTER THREE

# Making It Reliable

*When we practice*
*Embodying Something Repeatedly*
*we get better at it. And soon it is a*
*Skill We Possess.*

Preparing a Piece for Performance, Six Phases:
Step 3. REPETITION, MAKING IT MORE RELIABLE
STRATEGIES to Solidify Accuracy
Step 4. GIVE IT TIME TO DIGEST

Just knowing how to play a piece is not good enough for performing. The best is to internalize the piece to the extent that we could play it even if we were not thinking about it.

*The following is from the Introduction of this book, but some people may have skipped that, so it bears repeating here.*

## "I Played It Better at Home"

Every music teacher has heard (hundreds of times for many of us) a bewildered student say in a lesson, "But I played it better at home." One teacher I know even has those words on a plaque hanging in her studio.

Why don't we always perform at our best? And how can we make it more likely that when we are in front of an audience, we *will* play, if not at our *all-time best*, at least in a way that we can feel good about it and even proud of?

Athletes work to improve their skills with the hope that on the day of the competition they will equal their best time or score and even surpass it. Likewise, as musicians, there are those performances when we surpass ourselves, but most of the time, we will be happy if our performances just go as well as we played it at home or in rehearsal.

Those of us who have performed under a wide range of conditions and venues have learned that we usually lose a percentage of what we *could* do when we are performing. Less-experienced performers may lose 70% of their skill level when in front of an audience.

As people grow more accustomed to performing and do it more frequently, they may only lose 10%. Seasoned musicians who perform multiple times a week may be performing at 100% of their skill level.

There are a few reasons we don't always perform at our best. First of all, we also don't always play our best when we are practicing at home either. If you have played a piece 100 times at home, and 80 of those times you made some mistakes, there is only a 20% chance that you will play it without mistakes the 101ˢᵗ time you play it, either at home or in front of others.

If you don't often play in front of an audience, and get a bit nervous, you will likely lose at least 50% of your skill level. Now your chance of playing that piece without mistakes in front of an audience is only 10%!

## Preparing a Piece for Performance, Six Phases:

1. Learning how the piece goes, creating your **sound idea.** You know how it goes and how you want to be able to play it.

2. Working on the piece enough that **you can play all the sections at the tempo** you would like to perform it.

3. Making it **reliable**. This involves playing it repeatedly. Getting it to the point that you can play it multiple times in a row without mistakes. The 1,000 times repetition of Dr. Suzuki is a good example of this.

4. **Giving it time to digest**. Different parts of our brains record memory in different ways. It takes time for an **imprint of competence** to transfer from one part of the brain

to another. Once it does, our playing of that piece becomes more reliable.

5. Being able to **play the piece under pressure**, when conditions are not ideal or when things are challenging.

6. Being able to play through the **entire program twice in a row,** in a way that you feel good about. This develops your stamina (both physically and mentally).

**When you have completed these steps, you are ready to perform!**

===

**STEP #1** was covered in Chapter 1.

**STEP #2** is basically learning how to play the piece. Some strategies were given in Chapter 2. Gaining the skills to play your piece is also probably what you will work on with a private teacher.

There are additional technical strategies in *Success with the Violin and Life* (Book 1 in this series).

## Step 3. REPETITION, MAKING IT MORE RELIABLE

Modern neuroscience has been able show us how different parts of our brains perform different functions, how parts of the brain work together, and how the heart and gut also "think" and send information to the brain. Musicians have known for centuries that repetition is needed to acquire reliable skills.

Science can now describe this by showing how neural pathways are constructed when we do something new. These pathways get reinforced and strengthened as we do an action repeatedly. Habits get created when we do things over and over.

With repetition, the directives to accomplish the action move from one part of the brain to another. The details of this process are beyond the scope of this book, but you can readily access that information if you would like to know more. Search for *neural plasticity*.

The important thing to remember is that **what we are striving for is to be able to perform certain actions with consistency.** If we consistently get the result we want, that gives us a measure of reliability.

One major difference between someone who is just starting out and a seasoned player is that the mature player is aware that just playing something a number of times and getting it right a few of those is not going to cut it.

The less advanced player might attempt to play a passage 10 times. If it works two or three times, they may think this is enough. The mature player demands of themselves to play the passage 10, 20, or 50 times **in a row** correctly. 100 times in a row is even better!

## === STRATEGIES to Solidify Accuracy ===

When working to make something reliable and consistent, it is important to **make it measurable**. The simplest way is to count how many times in a row you played it correctly. Set your goal and then write down each day what you are able to accomplish.

I devised a few little games to teach my students about this. This is how I did it with the young kids. For adults the number of repetitions was higher.

### Game #1: Get Them All or Start Over

- You have to play it correctly 5 times IN A ROW.
- If you mess up on #4, you have to start from #1 again.

## Game #2: Each Mistake = 2 More Repetitions Needed

Set a goal for the number of correct repetitions. If it is not correct, there are two needed to "erase it." You can, of course, make it a higher number for more advanced players.

*EXAMPLE: Goal is 10 correct repetitions.*

*The first 3 go well. Score is now 3. We need 7 more.*
*4th try is wrong. Ooops! Now we need 9 more...*

**Note:** Kids seem to really enjoy the two games above, probably because it is so obvious and concrete. When they achieve it, they can know that it has been achieved (and, of course, there is a lot of celebration when they do). It is nice when something is measurable, and it is a great feeling to be able to check off that box and know they got the goal. Hurray!

## Turn On Your Recording Device

If you are counting your correct repetitions, recording it is a good way to make sure you are not fooling yourself. I have noticed that people sometimes are not aware of the mistakes they have made by the time they get to the end of a section or piece. See the story in Chapter 5, *Breaking a Habit*.

You can use your mobile phone for this. There is no need for a high-tech recording.

### Logging In 100 Repetitions

By the time you have played something correctly 100 times, you should know it. It is like a pilot who logs in flight time, or a driving student who is required to drive a certain number of hours before getting a driver's license.

### The Satisfaction of Achieving a Goal

It is very satisfying when we reach an obvious arrival point like 100 times/day. Choosing a goal for successful repetitions of a difficult passage will train your body to be more consistent and also give you a sense of confidence you would not have had without doing that.

=== STRATEGY ===

## Developing Reliability, 100 times/day

The story below is about muscle training, but the concept equally applies to working on a particular passage or entire piece.

### Story: Gaining 4$^{th}$ finger Strength

Most people find that their little finger (4$^{th}$ for string players, 5$^{th}$ for pianists) is weaker than the others. I created an exercise to strengthen this finger on the violin.

The basic idea is for the finger to be trained in the way that we want it to function while playing. It needs to be nicely curved – with each knuckle bent – and to function as a whole (not just from one of the knuckles, but from the base of the finger).

The exercise has three stages. The first is, on the A string, tapping on E flat with the little finger while the 3rd finger holds on D (a half step). The 2nd stage is tapping E natural while the 3rd finger is on D#. The final stage is tapping on E natural while the 3rd finger is on D natural (a whole step).

One does not want to over do this at first because it could set off some tendinitis. I told my student, Diane, to begin working with this exercise, but to only do the first phase five times on each string and then stop. She could do it again later, but not repeatedly, as this was likely to strain her muscles.

Two weeks later, I asked Diane how she was doing with strengthening her 4th finger. "I am up to 100 times a day now!" she said. "I started with 5 times each string (= 20 times) and did it at the beginning of my practicing in the morning and again in the evening (= 40 times/day). Then I changed to 10 times on each string twice a day (40 x 2 = 80/day). Then I added 5 times at the end of practicing in the morning" (40 + 20 + 40 = 100/day).

Great! That was for stage one. Needless to say, with her great focus and determination, Diane was able to strengthen her 4th finger quite quickly. She was delighted!

## Step 4. GIVE IT TIME TO DIGEST

Memories are stored in different ways in our brains. Short term memory is different from long term memory.

Good cooks know that certain foods taste better if the flavors have a chance to blend. When they marinate meat, they allow time for the flavors to really absorb. Likewise, we also play best when a piece has had time to "marinate" and sink in a bit.

What I have found during my years of teaching is that people usually need to be able to play their piece well at least one month before the recital. During that last month, they can solidify it with the techniques described in Chapter 4. If they can't play their piece well a month in advance, there could be some unhappy moments at the recital.

The next chapter will go into Step #5, *Making It Solid Under Pressure* and Step #6, *Stamina – Maintaining Focus & Endurance.*

CHAPTER FOUR

# Making It Solid Under Pressure

## Playing Well When Conditions Are Not Ideal

Step 5. WAYS TO SOLIDIFY A PIECE
Step 6. STAMINA – MAINTAINING FOCUS and
    ENDURANCE

### Skating on Thin Ice

When I was a kid, we looked forward to freezing weather because it meant the ponds would freeze and we could go skating. But we couldn't skate until the ice was thick enough. If ice is 2" thick or 12" thick, it looks smooth on the surface, but if you put weight on thin ice it breaks; thick ice will hold weight.

This is a good metaphor for performing a piece of music. We first get to a point where we can play the piece (the pond looks smooth and frozen), but then we need to solidify the piece (we need to be able to play it under pressure).

Unexpected things can come up in a performance, and we need to be able to continue despite the challenges.

**What kinds of kinds of things could come up?**

- Something distracts me; I lose concentration for a moment.
- I feel intimidated or get nervous when I perform.
- I am in a different environment – in my teacher's studio or on a concert stage, instead of at home where I practice.
- My health is not good – I could have a cold, a fever, a broken leg, a sore back, aches or pains.
- I have had an emotional shock – someone died, a relationship ended, I had an argument, someone insulted me or said something hurtful to me.
- I feel uncomfortable or strange wearing my concert clothes.

**Any of the above challenges will test the solidity of the piece.** They could crack the ice if it is not thick enough. If the ice is thick, we will still be able to function and play the piece well. If it is not, things are likely to go wrong.

# Step 5. WAYS TO SOLIDIFY A PIECE

- DIFFERENT TEMPOS
- DISTRACTIONS
- MAKE A RECORDING – Sound, Video
- PLAYING IN FRONT OF A PRACTICE AUDIENCE

## DIFFERENT TEMPOS

Your piece will be much more solid and you will play more musically if you are not restricted to just one tempo. You should be able to play it well at both a faster and slower speed. Use the metronome to keep you honest.

## Remaining at Ease

When you play your piece in the faster tempos, you are not trying to give yourself the feeling of playing FAST, you are playing it at a faster tempo and continuing to feel **comfortable and in control of things**. It is never a good idea to practice feeling rushed or out of control.

Likewise, you should have the presence and control to be able to slow it down. Don't let your body dictate the speed of the piece for you (like playing faster to avoid running out of bow).

## Having Control at a Slower Tempo

The way our bodies gauge time is by the beating of our hearts. That rhythm is our own private drumbeat or metronome. When we are nervous, our hearts beat faster. Therefore, playing your piece at exactly the same metronome speed you played at home will probably feel slower to you in performance.

Also, just because your heart is beating faster does not mean your fingers have the ability to play the piece at a faster tempo. This can create what musicians call a *train wreck*.

A faster-beating heart also means that you could distort the optimal tempo for the music by playing it faster than you would want to hear it if you were sitting comfortably in the audience.

So, playing it slower without speeding up (use the metronome) will help you a lot with maintaining control during your performances.

## Revealing the Musical Layers

Playing your piece at drastically different tempos will also give you the benefit of enhancing your musicality. When you play much faster or slower (for example at half tempo), you will notice different things about the piece. In a way, it is like a doctor looking at a biopsy of a tumor under a microscope.

It reveals more information about what was happening there.

So being able to play your piece at multiple tempos is good preparation for your performances. When we play more slowly, there are details that reveal themselves to us. Much faster gives us the overarching sense of what is being expressed. **All of it gives us a closer intimacy with the music we are playing.**

## DISTRACTIONS, While Still Playing with Ease and Accuracy

If you can play a piece with all sorts of additional challenges, that will make your ability to play your piece more solid. For each of the following suggestions, your goal is to be able to play the piece in an easy and accurate way.

### Types of Challenges:
- Body Position
- Bow Hold (string players)
- Distracting Sounds
- People Sitting Too Close
- Lights in Your Eyes
- Walk, Dance, Move Your Body
- Clothing
- Different Locations

### === STRATEGY ===

## Using Distractions to SOLIDIFY a PIECE

Play in an easy tempo. You will probably need to use the metronome to "keep you honest" with the tempo. It is easy to start speeding up when we know something very well.

If you make mistakes, play it again without the distraction. Then try it with the distraction again. Keep working on it until you can play it with the distraction and still play with ease and without mistakes.

## Body position: Play the piece with your body in different positions.

EXAMPLES:

- Standing with one foot on a chair
- Sitting on the floor
- Lying on the floor
- Balancing on one foot
- Sitting on something low or high
- Sitting with your feet up
- Leaning against something

## String Players: Hold the bow in a different way.

*EXAMPLES:*

- Reverse the bow and hold it near the tip
- Hold the bow in your fist
- Hold the bow farther up the stick nearer the balance point
- Use only the middle two fingers and thumb on the bow
- Put your thumb on the underside of the frog, instead of on the stick

## Distracting Sounds

People in your family can have fun with this one. They can:

- Clap at an unexpected moment
- Start telling the player a story
- Laugh or sing
- Turn on the radio and sing along loudly, dance and clap
- Make weird sounds, then laugh hysterically

**If you don't have anyone to distract you, you can:**

- Put on some other music that will distract you
- Watch a television show or movie while playing

### *Story: Just Running the Bartok Concerto*

A friend was at a summer camp for musicians. Through the door of the room across the hall she heard someone quite advanced playing the violin or viola. There was also a TV just blasting at the same time. What was going on?

Her curiosity got the best of her. She knocked and one of the most advanced students came to the door with her viola and explained, "Oh, I am just running the Bartok Concerto. If I can play through from memory while following the plot of a movie, I know I've got it down solid."

===

## People Sitting Too Close

Ask someone to sit or stand very close to you, watching your every move. They can even react dramatically to what you are doing.

## Lights in Your Eyes

When we perform on stage there are lights that will be directly on us. Positioning different bright lights that shine in your eyes or create a shadow on your music (so it is hard to read) is a good way to prepare yourself for what it will be like on stage. Turn off the lights in the rest of the room so that the effect is more like it would be in a concert.

## Walk, Dance, Move Your Body

Think of marching bands or Irish step dancers. Devise some of your own movements to do while you play.

- March to the music
- If your piece is in 3, do a waltz as you play
- Imagine you are a strolling violinist at a restaurant and seducing the restaurant patrons with your charms.

## Clothing

Be sure to play your music a number of times wearing the shoes and clothing that you intend to wear in an upcpoming performance.

CLOTHING CHALLENGES:

- Heavy winter boots
- Sunglasses (this is a very good one)
- Outdoor jacket
- Baseball cap
- Wide-brimmed hat (this is especially good because it will change the way your instrument sounds to you)
- Winter ski cap
- Wearing a scarf or shawl
- Your concert clothes and shoes!

## Getting Comfortable in Your Concert Clothes and Shoes

If you are planning to wear high heels, it is good to wear those while practicing your recital pieces. Your posture will be different than when you are in your bare feet or running shoes.

As you play, move your weight from foot to foot to keep your posture flexible and free. One young man used to ride the subway in his concert clothes so that he would feel more comfortable wearing them during concerts.

## Different Locations

Part of what can be intimidating about performing is being up on a stage. Being able to play your piece in odd places can help with this.

Suggestions:

- Play in every room of the house
- Play outdoors
- Play in the garage
- Stand on the stairs or the landing between stairs
- Stand on a coffee table or bench
- Stand in the bathtub
- Watch yourself play in the bathroom mirror

- Play in an empty recital hall or other place where concerts are held or the largest space you have access to
- Turn off lights and play in the dark.

## Coming Up with Creative Distractions Can Be Lots of Fun

Many kids who come for lessons with their parents or other siblings have fun with the distractions. Younger siblings enjoy coming up with new challenges for their older brother or sister, and it is a great feeling for the player to be able to triumph over a new challenge. "I can even play it lying down!"

To add a bit more suspense to the game, the ideas can be put on slips of paper and pulled out of a jar.

Below is a story that shows the importance of being able to play under many different conditions.

### *Story: Iiiiiiizzzzzzzzzz-zzzzz-zzzz!*

For a number of years, I played in a trio that provided classical music for formal parties and weddings. We were pleased to be hired for a job playing at the elegant Rosecliff Mansion in Newport, RI. The bride was an anchor woman for a television news show, so there were people with large television cameras recording the whole event. Along with the cameras came an elaborate array of stage lights that were carried on poles out to the back lawn where the wedding ceremony took place.

They could not have asked for a more picturesque setting with the wide lawn edged by rocky cliffs and the open ocean beyond. Behind us was the imposing mansion with its manicured gardens. The tasteful wedding decorations augmented its already regal elegance on this special day.

Or special evening, as this, being a Jewish wedding ceremony, was scheduled to begin just after sunset.

As the sun was setting, we played trios by Mozart and Haydn while the guests assembled. When we got the signal, we started the processional. There were a number of people in the wedding party – children, bridesmaids and groomsmen, two sets of grandparents, the groom and his parents and finally the bride with her parents.

Each set of people began at the mansion, processed down the terrace steps, walked across a flat area, then up another set of steps, a short walk and then down more steps to the lawn. Then there was quite a distance across the lawn to where we all were waiting. Giving each set of people their time in the spotlight, the next set would wait inside the mansion until the previous set had processed all the way to the front.

The grandparents were not as spry as they probably once were. And our processional music became an endless loop as we repeated the various sections over and over. In 20 years of playing weddings this was the longest processional by far!

Meanwhile, dusk had set in and our stage lighting sent out an all-points alert to every mosquito within a 2-3 mile radius. "Come to the wedding, bare flesh available and people unable to slap."

The mosquitos were biting my arms, neck, face, ankles, hands, fingers... the fingers were the worst part. I now had the music memorized, so could watch as the mosquitos landed on my fingers and filled up on my blood. I felt like my whole body was a mass of bites, and there was nothing I could do to stop them.

Not to complain because the flutist had it worse. They landed on her lip while she was playing and bit her there. When she inhaled quickly to grab a breath between phrases, a mosquito met its end as it went into her mouth.

Finally, finally, the bride and her parents arrived – at long last! I was able to cover as much of my body as possible while we waited it out through the ceremony. Meanwhile the stage lighting had shifted away from us and was centered on those in the front.

The young starlets (the bridesmaids) sat in front of the television cameras with their classic black velvet dresses – bare shoulders and arms with much of their backs exposed as well. I marveled at their self-controlled poise in front of the cameras as I (no longer in the spotlight) swatted mosquitos as discreetly as possible.

There was one more challenge when at last the recessional came. As the wedding party left, the stage lighting which had provided lighting for the whole affair, left along with them. We finished our work that evening playing from memory in the dark.

Later during the cocktail hour, there was some comic relief as a guest related to us in an unfettered Texan drawl that he had watched as a mosquito landed on the back of one of the blond starlets in the bare-shouldered dresses in front of him. "I was watching as it landed on her and just sucked that blood right up. I didn't know whether to slap her or what!"

Moral of the story: A professional needs to be able to perform even when the conditions are not ideal.

===

**Two other important ways to solidify your piece are:**

• PLAYING IN FRONT OF A PRACTICE AUDIENCE
• MAKING A RECORDING – Sound, Video

These will both be covered in Chapter 7, *Dealing with Nerves*.

# Step 6. STAMINA – MAINTAINING FOCUS and ENDURANCE

When we are playing a solo recital with multiple pieces on the program, there is an added challenge – maintaining our focus and strength throughout the whole performance.

You have probably had the experience of "zoning out" when you were driving and missing a turn or exit. What happened? The mind got focused on something other than following the route to the destination.

Driving is similar to playing an instrument in that it happens in real time, it's continuous. The optimal is when we are consistently alert and aware of what is happening and we are operating skillfully. Driving accidents happen, and that is also true when we are performing. Often what that means is that there was a loss of focused attention. Our minds went off track for a moment or more.

How to avoid such things when performing a solo recital for 90+ minutes? We are the ones there in the spotlight. *That spotlight remains on us.* It's up to us to remain fully focused in each moment. No vacation time here.

I had a friend in college that wrote a song, "When your mind is on vacation, but your mouth is doing overtime." That's not what the audience came to hear!

Because personalities are so different – certainly the way people think in their minds is unique to them – each one of us will find our own way with this challenge. However, below are a few suggestions for your consideration.

## Developing Endurance

It is definitely worthwhile when preparing for a recital, that we begin doing a nonstop run-through of our program at least once a day for many days (preferably weeks) before the actual performance. This gives both our muscles and minds a chance to develop the strength that will be needed to continuously maintain a high level of competence and skill throughout the whole program. The only way to develop this is by doing it repeatedly.

If you record these sessions and then listen to them later (maybe while driving or exercising) you will get a lot of added benefit. You'll hear things you like and don't like, and also pick up on places where you were not as strong.

## Developing Extra Strength

Athletes know that to perform at their optimal level they need to fill their well of strength to a level that goes beyond what they will need to compete. Likewise, if we have the strength (both physical and mental) to **play through our entire program twice in a row,** that is a good indicator that we have it in us to make it through a performance.

**Note:** When I played in the backup orchestras for traveling popular stars like Ray Charles and Paul Anka, we did two back-to-back performances each night, and also had a rehearsal in the afternoon. So that was not just a way to prepare, that was what we actually had to do.

## Transitions

Those run-throughs also train us in the transitions of going from one piece to the next. There could be key changes, stylistic changes, dynamic changes, meter and tempo changes…

This is also true of the transitions within each piece – one movement to the next and sections that repeat. The transitions are often a weak point that people tend to under-rehearse.

Whatever we hear gets immediately compared to what we heard just before that. This happens on the small scale in the relationship of each note to the next, but it is also happening on a larger scale. If the last movement ended double forte and the next movement begins very softly, that has a different feeling than if the next movement continues with the loud dynamic of the previous movement.

There is an interesting TED talk with Beau Lotto that shows how our eyes see colors very differently when the same color is surrounded by a different set of colors. This is also true for sound. **Everything we perceive is in a context,** and that context contributes a lot to what we perceive.

## Meditation and Mindfulness

If it suits your nature, working with various meditation techniques or mindfulness exercises can help train your brain to maintain a focus for longer periods of time. Once your brain has been trained in this way, you will be able to apply those skills to your performing as well.

## In the Zone, Becoming the Music

Athletes, musicians, writers, dancers, and artists of all sorts can have the experience that has come to be called "Being in the Zone." When we enter this state, the totality of *who and what we are* is focused and both "riding" and immersed in a flow that is so seductively wonderful that we are not interested in anything that is *not that experience*. In that state, we don't lose focus because there is nowhere else we would rather be.

Of course, we would like it if each time we played, we were *in the zone* and that it lasted for the entire performance. Unfortunately, it doesn't usually work out that way. However, the more we are in love with the music itself, the more likely it is that we will go into this. But again, this is probably so personal that the doorway into this state will be unique to each of us.

CHAPTER FIVE

# When Mistakes Happen

## Staying Focused and Keeping Going When Mistakes Happen

### STOPPING ALONG THE WAY TO FIX MISTAKES

This is the "I'll just stop and fix that" or "I didn't get that right, I'll do it again." It is natural to do this, but **it can become a disability.** The disability is that the person cannot play through the piece without stopping.

It is an easy habit to get into. We hesitate, stop or repeat something that didn't work, even though we had planned to do a run-through as though it was a performance. We change our minds (after all, it's not really a performance…).

This is a tough one to fix once it has become entrenched. Here are two strategies to work on this problem.

### === STRATEGIES ===

## If You Stop to Fix Mistakes

*Strategy #1: Don't Stop Exactly Where It Happens.*
**FINISH THE PHRASE, and then Go Back and Fix It.**

The reason we do it, is that we want to make sure we have everything working well. Just plowing through and making loads of mistakes leads to pretty slopping playing, so we DO want to correct things as they come up. The difficulty comes because a person can lose the ability to keep going – even in a performance.

We can avoid this problem by simply always continuing and finishing the phrase or section we are playing. **Regardless of the mistakes, keep going until the end of the phrase. Then stop, go back and work out whatever is needed.**

That way we still correct errors and reinforce our ability to play it right, and at the same time we strengthen our ability to push on through when there are difficulties.

During the bulk of their practice time, most people are working on improving or perfecting different spots. Strategy

#1 would be used during that time. That is different than playing it as though it was a performance.

In a performance we need to keep going, even if we are not happy with how we just did something. If you are having trouble doing that, here is a suggestion.

### Strategy #2: Getting Through a Whole Piece Without Stopping or Repeating

1. Put the metronome on an easy tempo.

2. Resolve that you will keep going no matter what.

3. **Turn on your recording device.** This is a way not to fool yourself by forgetting that you repeated something or hesitated.

It becomes so second nature that people actually forget they have stopped or repeated. The power of our minds to overlook what we do not want to remember is strong.

4. Play all the way through, keeping pace with the metronome. Using the metronome keeps you honest.

5. Listen to the recording and make notes on the music where the problems occurred.

### Story: Breaking a Habit

A 10-year old student had fallen into the habit of stopping each time she missed a note or rhythm and doing it again to get it right before she continued. This was probably her basic mode of practicing at home.

In the lesson I asked her to play it as though it was the recital now (no stopping). She started out with great resolve, but soon she was stopping and fixing without even thinking. When she reached the end of the piece I asked her how many times she thought she had stopped and started something again.

She hesitated, "One, or maybe two?"

"Five."

"Really?"

"Yes."

We needed to find a way to fix this. She was a very bright kid, was responsible, and had a great attitude. She was sure she could fix this. She said she would show me she could do it next week, so I didn't push it.

Next week the same problem. This time it was agreed that when she practiced at home, she would use the metronome to help her keep going. She PROMISED she would get it for the following week. But the next week it was still the same.

We needed to employ a different strategy. I decided to try the Reward/Loss system.

I put 6 quarters on the music stand. "These are all yours now, but each time you stop you will lose one of them."

The effect was magical. I only needed to reach over and take a quarter off once. The second time she began to stumble I started to reach out my hand to take another one. When she saw the hand coming, she pushed her way through without stopping.

When she finished we celebrated and laughed about when I reached out to take the 2nd quarter and she became even more determined.

I really meant it when I said she could have the quarters that were left, but she refused to take them. I don't think the money itself was what made the difference. The money was just an obvious symbol of what was happening, and using it made it a clear challenge.

We talked about what would be the best way for her to be able to have the same success repeatedly at home. She volunteered that they could use her allowance as the money she would lose. I was surprised, but she wanted to do it that way. She really did have a strong desire to play it well.

When the recital came she was able to play through her piece without hesitations, and she did a great job. Hurray!

# CHAPTER SIX

# Memorizing Your Music

GENERAL: Starting Anywhere in the Piece
1. AUDITORY MEMORY – Remembering the Sound
   SPEEDING UP YOUR SOUND-MEMORIZATION
   SUBCONSCIOUS LEARNING -- Passive Listening
2. VISUAL MEMORY – Remembering the Printed Music
3. MUSCLE MEMORY – Remembering the Fingering and Bowing
4. Using ASSOCIATION to Aid Your Memory

When you have been away and start driving back home, the closer you get to where you live, the more familiar it all is – the more you have a mental picture or idea about what you expect to see around the next corner.

Likewise, when we are playing a piece of music, the more familiar we are with it (the more it is embedded in our memories) the more we can be sure of what is coming up in the music. So if a piece is memorized, we have a more thorough connection with it, and we will "know it" better.

We can pace ourselves in leading up to the next climax or poignant moment; we will gauge our tempos better; the more our musical phrasing and pacing will make sense; and the more comfortable we will be with the notes.

Whether we choose to use the printed music or not in performance, if we cannot remember how a piece sounds, how can we possibly have a clear *sound idea* of what we are intending for a piece of music?

In short, the more clearly it is memorized, the better we will play it.

## THREE MODALITIES FOR MEMORIZATION

There are three basic modalities used for memorizing music – *auditory*, *visual* and *muscle memory*. Each one of us will find that one type comes to us more easily, so it is easy to depend on just that one way.

However, if we combine all three of these modalities, our ability to remember something becomes much more solid. If *association* is included, it is better yet.

# GENERAL

## *Being Able to Start Anywhere in the Piece*

One common mistake made by students and amateurs is to always start at the beginning of a piece.

This is like the woman who insisted that the only way to find a letter in the alphabet was to start at the very beginning of the Alphabet Song and sing all the way through until she reached the right letter.

I worked in a library and was assigned the job of shelving books which were in alphabetical order by author. I learned the alphabet in sections and where each section fit. If every time I shelved a book, I had to sing from the beginning of the Alphabet Song for every letter in the author's name, I never would have gotten my work done.

> ***Always starting at the beginning
> wastes a lot of time.***

## 1. AUDITORY MEMORY

### *Remembering the Sound*

As musicians, many of us tend to be more sound-oriented than other people. We recognize people by the sound of their voices, and we sometimes listen more to the timbre and inflections of their voices than to the words they are saying. Their voices tell us what they are really thinking and feeling, so it is the sound of the voice that tells us if the words are credible or not, and what is really going on.

Likewise, when getting acquainted with a new piece of music, we remember the sound of it more than how the notes look on the page or which finger played each note.

### *Story: A Break in Memory When a Piece was Memorized Using Only Auditory Memory*

Derek goes out on the stage to play his first piano recital. He starts out just fine, but suddenly loses it and needs to stop.

The only way he can get it back is to go all the way back to the beginning and start over. It is as though the audio recording "ribbon" inside his head was cut. Once that stream is broken, he is left adrift and completely lost.

===

If, along with the sound memory, Derek had also developed a visual and muscle memory of the piece, he would have been able to access those other ways of remembering and continue, maybe just moving forward to the next section.

## "I can't memorize music."

Sometimes new students will come for lessons and say that they cannot memorize music. What this usually really means is that they do not yet have good AUDITORY memory. These students will still be able to memorize music if they use their visual and muscle memory.

## Developing a memory for sound

They can also develop their auditory memory by choosing one piece of music and listening to it hundreds of times. Eventually they will remember the succession of sounds that make up that piece. Once they have memorized the sound of one piece, they will then more readily memorize others.

## 1,000 Repetitions

Dr. Shinichi Suzuki found this to be true when he taught young children haiku. He found that every child, even those with difficulty learning, were able to remember a haiku after 1,000 repetitions.

After memorizing the first haiku, they needed far fewer repetitions to memorize the next one. Soon all the children could remember a new haiku after only hearing it a few times. They had developed *the ability to remember* by learning the first few haiku.

The reason most people think they are not capable of remembering is that they have never invested in the first 1,000 repetitions.

## Developing a "Sound Memory" of a New Piece

A Sound Memory of a new piece is developed by:

- **Hearing it many times, repetition**
- **Focusing on it deeply and completely, heightened focus**

## Repetition

Building on what he had learned from teaching the children haiku, Dr. Suzuki utilized repetition to achieve auditory memory in his Suzuki Violin Method. He referred to it as the "mother tongue method."

Students listen to recordings of the pieces they will play many times before learning to play them. That way an inner recording is already embedded in their minds before they attempt to play each piece. When the kids learn this way, they are able to play pieces that are much more advanced and complex than if they were learning those pieces by reading.

## Heightened Focus

### Focusing on it deeply and completely

When something has a big impact on us, our senses go on high alert and the experience makes a profound imprint in our memories. Advertisers have studied ways to do this because they want the audience to remember the product they are selling.

Some ways to impact people are: sudden sounds, rapid motion, and/or something with emotional impact, like basic desires, cravings or fears.

These methods are not something you are likely to be using when you are memorizing a new piece of music; however, if a piece of music deeply moves you or impresses you in some way, you will remember it much better.

## SPEEDING UP YOUR SOUND-MEMORIZATION

To maximize your results, use both conscious and subconscious learning methods.

### CONSCIOUS LEARNING METHODS -- Active listening

- **Listen giving it your undivided attention.**

Stop doing anything else and just listen to the music. See if you can pick out the main melodies and the form of the piece. Notice which parts you like the most. Look forward to hearing them as they come up in the piece. Focus only on listening and try not to let your thoughts stray to anything else. If possible, move the recording back to an earlier place in the piece each time you realize that you have lost your focus.

- **Follow the printed music as you listen.**

Sit with the printed music and follow along while you listen. Tapping the rhythms on the notes as they go by will bring added benefits. Singing along as you listen to a recording is also a big help.

- **Sing it back.**

When learning a short section, listen to it and then sing what you just heard.

## SUBCONSCIOUS LEARNING -- Passive Listening

- IN MOTION
- AT REST

### Entering a Receptive-Learning State

There are a number of ways to enter into an enhanced, learning-receptive state. People enter into states of light-trance a number of times each day without even being consciously aware of it. Did you ever find you missed an exit on the highway, or looked down at your watch and wondered where the time went?

People are different when it comes to what helps them relax. Some people are more relaxed when they are moving, others when they are not.

### Passive Listening – IN MOTION

If you relax more easily when you are in motion, below are some suggestions. It works particularly well if the activity you are involved in is repetitive and not difficult. It also helps if there is a quiet atmosphere around you.

### In the Background

Set up a recording of your piece to play repeatedly. When we used tape recorders, we could get endless-loop cassettes for this purpose. Now you can set an auto-repeat function on your mobile device (you may need to put it in a separate folder so that only this one piece repeats).

**As the recording of your piece plays repeatedly:**
- Go about doing your daily chores or housework
- Use an exercise bike, treadmill or a rowing machine
- Do yoga or Tai Chi
- Go out for a walk, listening on your mobile device

## Passive Listening – AT REST

If you feel more relaxed and at ease when you are sitting or lying down, here are two suggestions for entering a light-trance state where you will learn easily and quickly.

For both suggestions below, set up a recording of your piece to play repeatedly while you relax into a highly receptive state of accelerated learning.

## • Relaxation Techniques:

Possibilities: taking a hot bath, sitting outdoors and watching the wind in the trees, lying in a hammock, swaying on a porch swing, rocking in a rocking chair. To go deeper you can stare at the ceiling, and when your eyes tire, let them close. There are also a number of different relaxation methods that involve using the breath.

- **Here are a few calming breath methods.**
*These are also repeated in Chapter 8.*

When we feel anxious, we tend to breathe more rapidly and with shallow breathing. A good way to counteract this tendency is to breathe slowly and deeply, filling your diaphragm (not just your lungs/chest). It helps to clear your lungs as much as possible first. Blow out as far as you can or sing a long note until there is absolutely no breath left. Then try one of the breathing patterns below.

**1. Counting** is the most common technique, but there are many variations of that. You can try different ones and see what works out the best for you.

IN-2-3-4, rest, rest, OUT-2-3-4, IN-2-3-4... (the rests are waiting) or IN-2-3-4, OUT-2-3-4, rest, rest, IN-2-3-4...

2. As above with the IN through your nose and OUT through your mouth, like gently blowing out a candle.

4. Breathe IN with eyes closed, OUT with eyes open, releasing any busy thoughts.

5. Put your attention on the sensations as the air comes in and out of your body while breathing normally (without attempting to change it in any way).

6. Alternate nostril breathing. Block one nostril, breathe out and in through the other nostril, then switch.

## 2. VISUAL MEMORY

### Remembering the Printed Music

Some people are gifted with what is called *photographic memory*. When they read something or look at something closely, a visual imprint is made in their memory. Once they have read a certain passage, they can later recall that passage by simply "reading it" in their minds.

Most people have this ability to a lesser extent and use it without even thinking about it.

*EXAMPLE*: Many of us use visual memory when we are driving and remembering where to turn. We look for landmarks and then remember how things will look when we turn left or right.

*EXAMPLE*: If you read something in a book and later you are trying to remember where it was, you may know what part of the page it was written on.

**Note:** Some people visualize things by "knowing" what is in their mind's eye, rather than actually seeing it as a picture in their minds.

## BENEFITS OF VISUAL MEMORY

### Knowing where you are in the piece

Visual memory can be like a map that shows us where we are in a piece of music. As we play, we can see where we are on the page and what comes next.

For example, when playing a piece in Rondo form (ABACA, ABACABA or similar), the "A" section repeats a number of times throughout the piece.

If we have a visual memory of where we are on the page, we know which "A" section we are playing. If we have only a sound memory of the piece, we may play the wrong section after one of the "A" sections.

Suzuki teachers use a form of this when they teach kids using the "Twinkle Sandwich" – "Bread-cheese-cheese-Bread" for "A-bb-A." This works for Twinkle, May Song, and other songs.

The sections of a piece can also be laid out on the floor. The student then stands in front of each while playing it, then moves to the next.

### Getting back in if you miss something

Another advantage is that you will remember how each section starts and will be able to move ahead to it, getting back in if you miss something in the preceding section. If you make a mistake, the audience wants you to keep on going. They do not want to have to watch you start all over again from the beginning.

## DEVELOPING A VISUAL MEMORY OF A PIECE

*Here are two methods:*

### • Write Out the Notes

One highly effective method (which is, unfortunately, also pretty toilsome) is to sit and write out the notes of a passage you want to memorize. If you can do this, you will have a clear memory of what the notes are.

### • Seeing Where You Are in the Music

Another method, and one that works very well as an adjunct to using sound memory and muscle memory, is to work with seeing where you are in the music. This can be done easily and fairly quickly.

Excellent results are guaranteed if you just go through the steps methodically.

## === STRATEGY ===

## Steps to Seeing Where You Are in the Music

1. Put the metronome on at a comfortable speed. Play the section or piece that you want to memorize. Play it 3 times in a row correctly and with ease.

2. Step back about a foot and play it again. Be sure to keep your eyes on the music as you play, even if you remember how it goes.

3. Once you can play it easily 3 times in a row, step back farther and play it again.

4. Repeat, until the music is too far away for you to actually read the notes. At this point you will be seeing where you are on the page and remembering what is within the section you are playing.

## While doing this process, it is important to:

- **Play with ease.**

Never play in such a way that you tense up or strain. If you have trouble, just move forward again and play it until it becomes more solid.

- **Maintain accuracy in rhythm.**

As we get to know a piece better, it is easy to start speeding up unintentionally. If you want to play faster, move the metronome up but keep everything rhythmically accurate.

- **Keep your eyes on the place you are playing.**

It is easy to stop actually looking at the notes as you begin to remember it, but for training the visual memory, it is important to keep your eyes following your location on the page of music.

## VARIATIONS on this method:

- If you wear glasses for distance, you can just take your glasses off.

- If you have access to a copy machine or scanner, make a series of copies in smaller versions – 90%, 80%, 70%, etc. You can also often set your printer to print it out at a smaller percentage.

This is especially helpful if you don't have enough room to move back far enough from the music stand. This would particularly be true for pianists.

# 3. MUSCLE MEMORY

## *Remembering the Fingering and Bowing*

The most effective way to develop muscle memory is to play a piece hundreds of times. When our bodies have done something hundreds or thousands of times, we no longer need to guide it with our minds.

The body remembers and just does it without our needing to think about it.

## If your mind loses focus for a few seconds

Muscle memory can be a real blessing if we are performing and for a moment, our concentration drops or we get distracted. If we have played the piece enough times, the fingers and bow continue playing even without our mental focus.

Remember the violist running the Bartok Concerto in Chapter 4?

## Fast notes

Another time the muscle memory is particularly needed is when the notes are too fast for us to think of and plan each one individually. We can program them into the hand, so to speak, and then just flip the switch for that passage.

### Story: My Body Remembered What My Mind Forgot

In the string section of an orchestra, all the players should be synchronized in their bowing. If there are places played by all of the strings, the concert master will dictate what these bowings will be. Otherwise, it is up to each section leader (the 1st chair, called the "principal") to chose the bowings that will be used by their section.

I was the principal viola in an orchestra for 17 years. We would receive our music by mail a few days before the first rehearsal. There was a symphony I had not played before on an upcoming concert. When I received the music and began to play through it, an odd thing happened. There were some tricky places and my left hand already knew the fingering and played through them easily.

That was strange. What was happening? Then I began to look through the music more carefully and recognized my own handwriting on the bowings and even a few other markings. I *had* played this symphony before! My mind had forgotten, but my body had not!

This is a perfect example of how memory is stored differently in our thinking mind and our "body mind." How nice for me that my fingers remembered the difficult places in that symphony even though in my mind I did not remember having played it before.

===

## Developing MUSCLE MEMORY More Quickly

### A Short Forgetting Time

The first thing to understand is how the body forgets. It is not possible to do it all at once like cramming for an exam. The body does not learn that way.

After we do an action there is a period of time where the body remembers what we just did. A good example is when there are a series of notes that repeat many times in a row. The natural tendency is to speed up each time because it gets easier to play them each time (because we just did it).

If there is a series of notes that we played two hours ago, and now we decide to play them again, there will be *some* memory of doing that, but nothing like when we were playing it repeatedly.

The real key to teaching your body to do something is not so much how long you spend going over it, but rather how long the "forgetting time" is. **The shorter the forgetting time, the faster the body will embed a memory of how to do that action.**

When I taught beginners, the first skill they learned was the bow hold. I emphasized that the shorter the forgetting time (between when they did the action and the next time they did it), the faster it would become so natural they wouldn't even need to think about it. They would be able to just reach for the bow and their hand would automatically go into the proper bow hold.

Therefore, working on it for 30 minutes, once a day, would yield a very slow result. If they missed a day, it would be even worse. However, if they picked up the bow and did the bow hold and a few little exercises for 2-3 minutes, multiple times a day, they would learn very quickly.

First thing in the morning and just before bed were important because they would not be doing it while they were sleeping.

I had one student who had the bow hold completely solidified in just one week. It turned out that he watched a lot of TV. He had the bow on a table in front of him and each time a commercial came on, he did the bow hold and bow exercises. Presto! He had it down cold before the next lesson.

Below are some **ways to promote the muscle memory**. These will speed up the learning and reduce the number of times needed to instill this type of memory.

- **Tapping**
- **Finger Patterns**
- **The First Note of a Phrase or Section**

## Tapping

Go through your piece tapping the rhythms with a pencil in your right hand (bow hand for string players). Next, go through it again, this time tapping with the fingers on the left hand. This will help your body to remember the rhythms.

## Finger Patterns (string players)

Knowing the whole finger pattern (the spacings of all four fingers) will help you see the fingerings in groupings, rather than just individually.

*EXAMPLE:* If you are going to play a 2-octave scale all in one position, practice putting all four fingers down in the correct relationships, one string at a time. Know the patterns of whole steps and half steps for each string.

By putting all four fingers down at once as a unit, you will imprint your muscle memory with **that pattern as a unit**. It is now like a word, instead a series of random letters.

It is similar to how a ballet dancer has 1st position, 2nd position, etc. Each leg and arm are not remembered separately. The 1st position includes both arms and both legs and is remembered as one pose. You want the finger-memory to be that way, too – one *pattern-unit* on each string.

## The First Note of a Phrase or Section

Creating a clear memory of how we start each phrase and section is an essential part of having a solid memory of the piece. This includes both the right and left hands.

Being able to start anywhere is especially important when we are performing. If something goes wrong, we can start at the beginning of the next phrase. Mid-phrase is even better.

=== STRATEGY ===

## Steps for Training Your First Note Competence

**For the first note:**
- Which finger(s) do you play that note with?
- What is the name of the note or chord?
- What is the relationship of that note to both the preceding note and following note?

**Test yourself on each starting note.**

Go through the piece playing only the 1st note of every large section in the piece.

Then go through each section and test yourself that you can play the first note of every phrase in that section. Particularly important are the notes immediately after a rest.

# 4. USING ASSOCIATION to AID YOUR MEMORY

It is easier to remember things we are already familiar with. If we see something as resembling something familiar, that helps us remember.

## Attaching something known to something new

We can attach something we have already learned to something new. If my sister's name is Barbara and I meet someone new named Barbara, I think, "Oh, she has the same name as my sister." Making that association will make it much more likely that I will remember the name.

## Looking for patterns we already know

In music when we see scales or arpeggios that we already know, we can think of them like words that fit into the whole, instead of a series of individual letters.

When a beginning student first learns Twinkle, Twinkle Little Star and later learns May Song, realizing that the form of both songs is the same can make it much easier to remember what is coming up. "Oh, it is the same as the "Twinkle Sandwich – bread-cheese-cheese-bread" (the "A-b-b-A" form).

***EXAMPLE: Bach Double, "Pepperoni Pizza"— four 16th notes followed by two 8ths***

For a student who has learned using the Suzuki method, he might see the first movement of the Bach Double violin concerto as beginning with a scale, then jumping to the octave, and played with the "Pepperoni Pizza" rhythm. He is just putting a series of notes he already knows to a rhythm he already knows.

***EXAMPLE: Mississippi Reel***

The Mississippi Reel starts out with the rhythm "Pepperoni Pepperoni Pepperoni Pizza." Each "Pepperoni" is a descending scale. The "Pizza" is an octave. The second line is the same finger pattern on the D string, except the "Pizza" is two open A's. Seeing it this way makes it easy to learn that piece quickly.

**Note:**

Most of the information in this chapter is also included in the *Success with the Violin and Life* book. That book also includes a short section with suggestions on applying these methods to memorizing telephone numbers, multiplication tables, and street addresses.

# CHAPTER SEVEN

# Performance Nerves

- OVERALL APPROACH
- AVOID STIMULANTS
- HANDLING THE EXTRA ENERGY
- MAKE A RECORDING – SOUND, VIDEO
- PLAYING IN FRONT OF A PRACTICE AUDIENCE

Many of us have a certain amount of nervousness about performing. For some, it is so intense that we could call it stage fright. Even if we have worked hard to prepare our music, how can we ensure that we will be able to play it up to our own standard in a recital, concert or audition?

What keeps us from playing our best?

**1. Fear of Failure**

**2. Fear of Judgment/Criticism/Attack**

**3. Both!**

**Fear #1,** *Fear of Failure* is definitely set off when we don't feel confident in our own abilities. This is the difference between "I know I can do this," and "I hope I am lucky enough that it works this time and I don't mess up the way I often do."

**Fear #2,** *Fear of Judgment/Criticism/Attack* will be covered in Chapter 8. This is the fear that can bring on the debilitating stage fright that can be so hard to deal with.

# OVERALL APPROACH:
# Dealing with Nerves

### Be prepared. Know your piece well.

Knowing that you are not really well prepared can add a lot of fuel to a bit of nervousness. Give yourself the gift of having "done your homework." At least you will know that you have internalized your piece to the extent that you will be able to play it whether you are nervous or not. The techniques in Chapter 4 are good ways to help you achieve that end.

### *Story: Toastmasters. Many People Don't Know HOW to Prepare*

Toastmasters is an organization that helps people with public speaking. I participated in a local group and enjoyed the comradery and chance to work on my public speaking skills. We worked our way through a book that had a series of speech challenges. Each speech had particular goals and a limited time frame. Most of the first speeches were 3-5 minutes.

For my first speech, I worked out a topic and began by making an outline of what I wanted to cover. Next, I made a recording of myself giving the speech while looking at the outline. The first recording was 19 minutes. Ooops! That won't do.

So I pared it down to some essential concepts and made a new recording. Now it was down to 9 minutes. Better, but still out of range. Once I got it down to 5-6 minutes (each time recording myself speaking), I worked on speaking faster (did you ever notice how fast news commentators speak?). My goal was 4 minutes. That would give me some leeway, and take some tension out of worrying that I was cutting the time too close.

In order to do this, I needed to memorize the speech. Knowing exactly what I would say next, meant that I could speak much more quickly. I used some of the techniques from Chapter 6 to help me do this.

Soon I was ready to do my speech. The performance went well, although it was not quite as smooth as it had been at home.

When other people in the group went to deliver their speeches, some of them had to stop part way through because they were out of time. They had not tried timing it with a recording and just hoped it would be about right. They also had trouble with their visual aids. It was obvious that at home they had not gone through it using the visual aids while they were standing up.

I felt for them as they got nervous and stumbled with things. Everyone was compassionate, but it was a pity. Their nervousness would have been greatly diminished if they had known *how* to prepare well for a performance. Not being musicians themselves, it was not a skill they could draw on to help with preparing their speeches.

## Blaming Nerves When It is Really Lack of Preparation

Many times, people seem to blame themselves for not feeling more comfortable when giving a speech or presentation. They think they have trouble controlling their nerves, when much of it is just simply not knowing how to set themselves up to be in a powerful position when they speak or play by doing some thorough preparation.

If you were uncomfortably nervous during a performance, it is worthwhile to investigate that afterwards. We can ask ourselves, "How well did I prepare for that performance?

Did I do all that I could do to solidify it and make it reliable?" (See Chapters 1-6).

If we start believing we can't play because of nerves, that idea can take on a life of its own and put ourselves in a no-win position. Doing that is really to shortchange ourselves and to unfairly lock ourselves into an "I can't" position. That doesn't help us at all.

## Likely Expectations

As was pointed out earlier, it is likely that you will lose a percentage of your skill level when you perform. For people who don't perform very often, they could lose 70%. For someone who performs a lot, it might only be 10%. For someone who is giving concerts multiple times a week, it might not be at all.

While you are performing, noticing that you are not playing as well as you had hoped can distract you from continuing to do your best. **Not being surprised when little irregularities emerge, and taking that all in stride**, is a better way to handle it. Just knowing, that in the performance, you may lose some of your skill, enables you to be easier on yourself when it happens. You can be happy if it works out to be at all close to what you feel you could have done. Know that the more you perform, the more likely it is that your "percentage" will improve.

## Familiar or New/Surprising

Even though we would like to be completely prepared for a performance, in reality, we can never be *fully* prepared because life is a continuous flow. No two moments are exactly the same. Each performance will be unique in its own way.

However, the more aspects of it that *are* familiar, the less nerve-wracking it will be.

*Examples:*

• **Check the venue.** If possible, play in the concert hall where the performance will take place. Also check the "green room" or wherever you will be leaving your case and outdoor coat. Find out where the restrooms are. Drive there a few days ahead of time so there isn't any added tension about finding where the hall is. On concert day, arrive at least one hour ahead of time.

• While practicing at home, **wear the clothes** you will perform in. What **shoes** you wear makes a big difference in your posture and how you carry yourself. Your feet are the foundations of your body. Will you wear dress shoes? High heels? The more you wear them while practicing, the more comfortable you will be during the performance.

• Going through all the **challenges in Chapter 4** are a big help with getting you used to dealing with the unexpected and unfamiliar.

## Story: Fire, fire!

One of my first solo recitals was in a concert hall that was near a fire station. Part way through my piece, an alarm went off over at the station. Not something I would have practiced being ready for, but there it was. I did stay focused and continued to play, thank goodness. Afterwards, all the comments were about how I was able to keep playing, not *what* I played. So it goes.

# AVOID STIMULANTS

## Story: A French Menu

I was playing in an orchestra on a concert tour in France. We had rehearsed the music for this tour extensively, so I felt very confident of it. I was not a principal player, so there wasn't any particular personal pressure on me. In each city we played the same program, so it was definitely a low-stress type of performing.

Before one of the concerts, some of my colleagues and I had a meal at a local restaurant. The only options were three different set menus. These included a number of courses, followed by dessert and coffee.

Not having been a coffee drinker for years, I would not have ordered coffee after my meal, but since it was included and smelled so good, I drank it. That evening I was a nervous wreck during the whole concert. I knew that there was no reason to be nervous, but my body had other ideas.

I learned my lesson with that experience. Thank goodness I was not playing a solo that evening.

===

You may not be affected by coffee or other stimulants in this way, but let this story be a heads-up to be extra aware about what you eat or drink before a concert or recital.

## To Eat or Not To Eat

Some people find that it is best not to eat at all before a performance. Others say it works best for them if they eat a lot of pasta or something else that has a calming effect on them. Each person's body is different.

It is worthwhile to experiment and find out what is the best for you. Athletes are very aware of this. You might find it helpful to read up on what they say works for them.

**Breathing Techniques** can also be helpful in calming our nerves. See more in Chapters 6 and 8.

# HANDLING THE EXTRA ENERGY

There is a Buddhist practice where a monk will try to antagonize another monk with insults and outrageous statements. That way the one being antagonized can learn to handle his emotions when they come up and to have mastery over them. Many of us didn't get such good training. Our parents and the other adults in our lives were often not very good at handling their emotions.

Emotions are powerful. They are the motivators for much of what we do, and they can push people to do things they normally would not think to do. There is a reason we have the term "crimes of passion."

Athletes, pilots, and people doing any kind of performing or competing, have to develop strategies that allow them to function well when their emotions are running high.

We each have our own personal pharmacy built into our bodies which produces our fluctuating body chemistry. Adrenaline, oxytocin, dopamine, serotonin… Neurotransmitters rush through us and create strong emotional experiences.

It can feel like it is happening *to* us, that it is completely outside of our control (even though it is our own bodies that are making them). It is as though we are swimming in a sea of emotional reactions that can be stormy or calm. How well are we at navigating through those?

With performing, we won't know how our body chemistry will react until we've tried it. For most people there will be more energy that starts flowing, but the only way to find out for yourself is to do it.

## Playing too fast

It is common that when our hearts start to beat faster and the adrenaline starts to flow, we start to play faster. Unfortunately, this can lead to what musicians call a "train wreck."

After a few train wrecks people learn that their impression of the speed they are playing can get distorted when they are nervous. To control it, they learn to play at a speed that feels slow to them but is probably the same speed they normally play the piece. See more at "Having Control at a Slower Tempo" in Chapter 5.

## Suggestions for Dealing with the Extra Energy

1. **Keep your sovereignty**; employ the power of your will and focus. This is your life. You are the one who determines this event's meaning and importance to you.

2. Let your focus be on **navigating to your goal** as you ride the energy that pours through. What is your intention for this piece of music?

3. **Don't pretend** an emotion does not exist, that you are not nervous, fearful, upset, etc. The emotions are part of the experience.

4. If possible, **channel the extra power** of the emotion in the direction that will serve you and help you to play even better. Many athletes and performers find that having that extra edge focuses their intent and enhances their power. One professional basketball player told me that he played best when he was angry.

**Like the Water Behind a Dam**

The potential energy is like the water behind a dam. You don't want it to spill over and be out of control. Floodgates need to be opened to allow that force to come through in a controlled way. If you are able to do this, the energy can still come through without creating destruction. If you try to hold it back or deny its existence, it will eventually spill over and cause trouble.

=== STRATEGY ===

## Get Your Heart Pumping

Do some vigorous exercise that gets you out of breath and gets your heart pounding. Then, play your piece as though you were performing it. No stopping to fix things. Remember to do a bow before and after you play. You want to replicate the concert conditions as closely as possible. So see the audience in your mind's eye and bow to them.

=== STRATEGY ===

## Get Angry

Think of something that really upsets you. If you get into a heated argument with someone in your household or if you see something on TV that really makes you mad, immediately try playing the music you are currently working on.

See how differently your body feels when the adrenaline is flowing. Make a recording so that afterwards you can check the metronome speed you played at. Was it faster than normal?

=== STRATEGY ===

## Imagine the Person You Would Most Like to Impress

Think of who might make you nervous. Maybe some new love interest, a person you admire, or a fierce competitor. Resolve that you have only one chance to show them what you can do. Make a video of yourself playing for them and tell yourself you will send it to them afterwards. You have only one chance to do this. No second recording. Only one.

The idea is just to put yourself under pressure so that you can notice what happens within your body chemistry. Think of what might challenge you enough that your inner pharmacy will shift into high gear.

**Knowing how to
ride the heightened energy of performing
is an art in itself.**

## MAKE A RECORDING – BOTH SOUND ONLY and VIDEO

We are lucky to have so many recording options now – mobile phones that shoot video and also have recording apps, digital recorders, cameras with video functions, camcorders, laptop web cameras. You probably have at least one of these. Use it to help you prepare for your recital or concert.

If you make a video of yourself playing your piece each day, you will be able to fix many things on your own, even without the help of a teacher. As you watch yourself playing, you will see and hear things you would not have been aware of otherwise.

If you get a good video or recording, you can keep it in an archive of your performances, too! Go ahead and upload it to YouTube so that other people can enjoy it as well. There is no need to make it a professional video. A video shot with someone's phone can get millions of hits, so don't use the idea that you need all the proper equipment as an excuse not to do this. Hit that record button!

## PRACTICE AUDIENCE

### Rehearsing in Small Time to prepare for the Big Time

A good way to approach playing in front of an audience is to move into it a bit at a time. My students prepare for our recitals by playing repeatedly in front of progressively larger audiences. First, they play for me as the teacher, then for their families, a stranger, more people, the dress rehearsal, and finally the recital.

**If you don't do any of the preparatory performances, you really are not giving yourself a good chance at doing your best when the big day arrives.** Not only do we need to practice our piece, but also to practice performing, if we are to be well prepared.

*PRACTICE AUDIENCES FOR KIDS:*

Be sure to do the entire Performance Routine including walking out and bowing before and after the performance. See Chapter 9.

- Play for each member of your household
- Play for neighbors or friends
- Play for coworkers or at your parents' workplace
- Play for Grandma over the telephone or via the internet
- Stuffed animals make a friendly audience

**FOR ADULTS**, you can ask people who live with you or someone who lives nearby to come and be your practice audience.

**Make it clear to them exactly why you are asking them to do this.** That will make it easier for them to play their role. If you don't explain, they may think you are trying to impress them or seek their approval. That isn't the point for these practice audiences.

This is not a "look at me, see what I can do." **The reason to do it is simply to *practice*,** to have the chance **to see how your body reacts** when other people are listening.

Be sure to do the entire Performance Routine including walking out and bowing before and after the performance. See Chapter 9.

### Story: A Teacher's Regret

After graduate school, I began teaching private violin lessons. I found that it was important to have my students play in a recital at the end of each semester. Without the goal of a performance, people lost their focus and their practicing time could lose its priority.

I particularly noticed this with the high school students when they were required at school to go through yearly adjudications and auditions for all-state orchestra. As soon as they had that clear goal and date, they got very focused and practiced much more diligently.

With end-of-semester recitals, I was aware that this experience could color their belief in themselves, especially anything in the future that involved standing in front of a group of people. It could be performing music, but it could also be presenting at a staff meeting or giving a lecture. These recitals were a training ground for their future endeavors.

For this reason, I went to great lengths to have their recital performances be successful in a way that would create a positive imprint that would continue for the rest of their lives.

One of the requirements I put into place was that the students needed to be able to play through the piece without any difficulties at least one month before the recital date.

During that final month, we also had multiple "practice audiences" come into the studio to hear them play. This way they got accustomed to playing in front of people they did not know. Everyone was also required to play in a dress rehearsal a few days before the actual recital.

Katie was a diligent student. She progressed in her music studies slowly and carefully. Her mother came with her to the lessons and sometimes accompanied Katie on the piano. Katie's mom was a highly competent woman with a high-level administrative job. Katie's first recitals all went like clockwork. All was well.

She progressed through the *Suzuki Violin* book and her next recital piece was the *Happy Farmer*. She was doing well with it and I expected that she would do well on the recital. However, her mother was unable to come to her last four lessons because of work responsibilities and she also had a business trip that meant she would not be back in time to play at the dress rehearsal.

This violated some of my rules about the recitals. I needed Katie and her mom (playing piano) to have the practice performances with the small audiences and also to do the dress rehearsal.

What was I to do? In this case, because Katie had always been so solid on her previous recitals, I bent the rules. I allowed them to arrive early for the recital and just do a run-through before the recital began.

What a mistake. When it was their turn to play, Katie (playing from memory) got confused about which section she was playing. This piece has sections that repeat but have slightly different endings. She repeated the section without changing the ending and then repeated again. Her mother was a bit nervous herself and not quick enough to change and compensate.

My heart sank as I watched Katie go absolutely pale. Her eyes widened and she began to shake all over. She was traumatized. I was so very sorry. It is situations like this that people process in therapy in years to come. I deeply regretted not sticking to the rules I had set up. There was a good reason I had made them that way.

===

I include this story as a way to illustrate the importance of giving yourself the chance to play your best by doing the preparations that make that most likely. If you do not prepare in these ways, you might be tempted to chalk it up to "I just get so nervous."

That gives yourself (and others) the idea that the problem is something to do with your emotional stability or psychological maturity. **That is selling yourself short on your own abilities.** The reality was, you were simply not adequately prepared.

Please, give yourself a chance to show both yourself and others that you CAN play in front of an audience in a way that you feel good about, even proud of. If you follow the steps laid out in this book, you will be giving yourself and the audience a wonderful gift.

In the next chapter, we go into the deeper difficulty of what is called "stage fright." This is not just nervousness, but an all-out FEAR that is much more severe. There are additional strategies for overcoming that.

# CHAPTER EIGHT

# Stage Fright

- **THE PRIMAL FEAR:** CROWD ATTACK, DEVASTATING JUDGEMENT/CRITICISM

- **WHO IS OUR AUDIENCE?**
  REALITY CHECK, THE AUDIENCE
  SELF-CRITIC

- **DEALING WITH THE FEAR ITSELF**
  FACING THE FEARS
  BREATHING TECHNIQUES
  STEP BY STEP: OVERCOMING FEAR

- **OTHER WAYS TO DEAL WITH FEAR**
  Hypnosis, Beta Blockers

- **KNOW THAT FEAR DOES NOT NEED TO STOP YOU**

## STAGE FRIGHT

Some researchers tell us that 73% of the population have a fear of public speaking. Others say it is one in four. Either way, it comes in higher on the phobia scale than fear of death, heights, snakes, or spiders. So if you experience the fear of performing in front of an audience, you are by no means alone in that! The researchers call it "public speaking," but that certainly includes playing an instrument as well.

In the previous chapter, it was stated that there are two major fears that create the difficulties in performing in front of an audience.

**1. Fear of Failure** can be largely subdued by doing a series of intensive preparations. These create a sense of knowing that you can do well under all kinds of circumstances. When your basic belief is, "I can do this no matter what," the fear that you will fail does not have the potency.

**2. Fear of Judgment/Criticism/Attack** can be lessened by doing the intense preparation work, but there is a whole other layer that needs to be addressed to gain power over the "demon" of stage fright.

"Demon" is a strong word, but I chose it deliberately here because that can be how it feels. It feels as though something else is doing this *to* us without our wanting it to happen.

So, what is it that creates these highly unpleasant situations? Why can't we just decide that *all is ok* and proceed with our normal way of playing, just like we do at home?

## Subconscious Mind and Logical Mind

If you have ever attended a stage hypnosis show, you may have witnessed something quite revealing about how our minds work.

There are volunteers who come up to the stage and the hypnotist puts them into a state of hypnosis using what are called "rapid inductions." Once in the hypnotic state, people do all sorts of things that are entertaining to the audience.

Toward the end of the show, the hypnotist may choose one of the participants and tell her that after they all come out of hypnosis, she will feel wonderful. However, if the hypnotist snaps his fingers, she will immediately feel the need to take off her shoes. This is called a "post-hypnotic suggestion."

When the hypnotist brings all the people out of hypnosis and they "wake up," he interviews them about how they feel. They all feel wonderful.

As they continue to sit there on the stage, the hypnotist then begins to tell the audience a story. At one point he says, "And it happened, (snap), just like that." When he snaps his fingers, the person to whom he gave the post-hypnotic suggestion leans over and begins taking off her shoes.

The hypnotist goes over to her and asks, "What are you doing? Why are you taking off your shoes?"

What does she say?

To the amusement of the audience, she gives some "reason" (that she totally believes) about why at that moment she needed to take off her shoes. The really remarkable thing is that whatever reason her mind has come up with is *what she really believes to be true.* If someone told her, "No, you are just doing that because the hypnotist told you to do it before," she would vehemently deny it.

"No," she would say. "It's because my foot felt uncomfortable," (or whatever the "reason" was her mind came up with). She also will get angry if someone challenges her on this.

Note that the immediate-anger response is a quick way to notice if the belief is one that comes from careful consideration (the frontal lobe of the brain) or from a hypnotic suggestion which the subconscious has taken in as fact.

Taking in a suggestion like this does not even need to come directly from a hypnotist when you are in trance. **Waking hypnosis** can also bring about beliefs like this. People are susceptible to these suggestions when they are relaxed, someone speaks with authority, and if the idea is repeated a number of times. Watching a news channel with a definite political slant can easily "brain wash" people who are relaxing in their lazy-boy chairs while watching it.

We are also more susceptible when we are shocked by something. You will notice that advertisers use sudden sounds as a way to put the people watching into a more suggestible state.

## Checking If We Have Taken On Beliefs Through Waking Hypnosis

The easiest way to check if what you believe is something you took on through *waking hypnosis* (from the TV, for example) or if it is a well-thought-out conclusion you came to after evaluating perspectives from multiple varied sources, is:

> When you hear someone say a statement
> that conflicts with your belief,
> do you feel an immediate animosity?
> **Do you immediately feel you want to attack?**

If so, it is coming from your primitive-brain center and is most likely something you picked up through *waking hypnosis* (this doesn't mean that your opinion is right or wrong; it is simply a way to find out *why* you believe this).

If instead, your opinion is from careful deduction (frontal lobes), **you will not be emotionally threatened by hearing a different point of view.**

You may not *agree*, but you will not feel *threatened* by another perspective. You may feel compassion that they are so misguided or you may have some other immediate reaction that is not an attack on that person.

## How Does Learning About Hypnosis Help with Stage Fright?

In order to change our fearful reactions to performing in front of an audience, it is essential to understand that our reactions are not coming from our logical minds. They are coming from the primitive part of our brains that are all about SURVIVAL. This is no laughing matter. This is about responding to **a perceived threat to our safety**.

Someone may have told you to just imagine that everyone in the audience is naked or something like that. If that works for you, bravo, keep it up. But for the great majority of people, just trying to use the logical mind to *think your way out of it* is not effective.

A better approach is to **find out the language of that part of your brain, including its agendas and beliefs about what will keep you safe.**

Remember that this part of your brain is all about **safety and survival**.

# THE PRIMAL FEAR: CROWD ATTACK, DEVASTATING JUDGEMENT/CRITICISM

## The Language of Your *Primal Brain*

Unlike your logical-thinking brain, the *primal brain* (this is what I will call it) makes broad symbolic interpretations. It sees a situation in a symbolic way and draws a conclusion from that. Learning about the behavior of animals can help us understand how our own primal brain works.

If you watch birds at a bird feeder, you have probably noticed that they are constantly on alert. If there is a sudden movement or noise, they will immediately fly away. Our primal brains are like this, too. That part of our brain is focused on staying alive (our safety, getting what we need to survive, etc.).

Let's look at what your primal brain sees when you walk out in front of a crowd of people. **You are on one side (the stage) and they are all facing you.**

Most animals will interpret someone facing them head-on as a threat or challenge for dominance. The fearful response of the animal is then either aggression or surrender/fleeing.

Add to this another important factor. **You are out numbered.** This is a direct threat to your safety. Have you ever felt that other people ganged up on you? You may have been physically attacked or just verbally abused or made fun of by someone who had the backup of the group. Being attacked by a whole group at once when you are alone is even more horrifying. It is rare that a person has not had some sort of experience with feeling attacked by others at some point in their lives.

Your *primal brain* remembers this. If a situation resembles something from the past, it will expect it to have the same result.

**So the simple act of walking out on stage and facing an audience is interpreted by the *primal brain* as a dangerous situation.** Messages are sent to the rest of the body to be ready to respond to an attack. The idea would be something like, "I will probably need to fight for my survival here. Get ready."

Another important thing to understand is that the *primal brain* does not do a lot of discernment about **the *degree* of threat**. Getting fired from your job is a threat to your survival, just as being attacked by a street gang in the city is. If someone criticizes you or makes fun of you, that is also an attack. The primal brain is on the lookout for any threat and will prepare your body to defend yourself or counterattack.

**Anything that you would find devastating
– either emotionally, physically, financially or mentally –
is just one thing, *a threat*.**

## Our Default Programming

When we get a new computer or phone, it comes to us with a number of default settings. For example, there will be some sort of image or pattern on the desktop or home screen. We may choose to leave it that way, or to change it.

When we are born, we also arrive with some "default settings." The way our *primal brain* evaluates being in front of a group of people (as described above) is one of them. But what if, from the very beginning when we are young children, we repeatedly have wonderful experiences each time we are observed by a group of people? Everyone cheers when we are able to stand and walk. Our parents proudly encourage us to show people what we can do and we receive enthusiastic praise and goodies each time we do.

An interesting interview with the Late Show host, Stephen Colbert, is a good example of this (although I do not personally know what his childhood was like). He said that the audience is what really gives him his energy during the shows. He even said that if before a show he feels ill, the moment he walks out and feels the energy of the audience, it is as though, as he put it, "the audience heals me." He never feels sick while he is on stage. That's how much he benefits from performing.

So for someone like that, the original default program of "beware of being alone in front of a group" has been rewritten to one that says, "when I perform in front of other people, I get all kinds of good stuff."

The default programming and our childhood imprints – many of which are even preverbal – create the beliefs our primal brains carry throughout our lives. Some people spend years in therapy working on changing their early imprints.

The good news is that the science of neuroplasticity is now showing us that *we can change our brains.* We don't need to stay stuck in the default programming we were born with or even the learned behaviors of our childhoods. Psychologists and psychiatrists have devised lots of different ways to work on making these changes. Of course, hypnotherapy would probably be at the top of anyone's list who has severe stage fright because **hypnosis** is a direct way to change our subconscious programming.

This book will not go into modalities you would do with a psychotherapist, but instead provide some context to better understand what is happening and also give you strategies that you can do on your own.

## WHO IS YOUR AUDIENCE?

Humans are social animals. We function in group configurations. Even if you live alone and do not socialize, you are still part of a community, a country, and the global human experience in this era of time. You share a language and some basic thought patterns with the culture you were born into.

You may think you are without human ties, but at any time the government could decide to build a road through what used to be your house, or create a dam in a nearby river that floods the area in which you now live. We are inextricably interconnected with other people.

Animals live within a dominance power structure. It is a given for them. They are constantly aware of where they fit in the "pecking order" or food chain. When a new pet is introduced to a household, that new pet's rank in relationship to the other pets will need to be established before they all can live in peace together.

The primal brain part of ourselves needs to know that, too. Where do I fit into the existing power structure here? Are the people around me allies or enemies, above me on the power scale or below me? Our logical thinking brain may like to believe that there is equality for all, but that isn't how our *primal brains* think.

So when we perform in front of an audience, our primal brains will need to know, **are they allies or enemies?** How much of a threat are we facing here?

## *Story #1, String Quartet*

I was playing in a string quartet that had an upcoming performance. The cellist suggested we have his teacher come to give us a coaching session. She was an older woman, very self-possessed and clear about what she thought would help us improve our performance. There were no extra words or conversation. She was all about getting right down to work.

What I found interesting was that our cellist suddenly played much better now that his teacher was listening.

Even though she was not all that warm and effusive, she was a definite ally. We all knew that she had high standards but was totally on our side. She wanted us to be able to play at our best. That came through in the effect she had on her cello student. In her presence, he was alert to what he was doing and focused on being the cellist she knew he had the potential to be.

## *Story #2, Beethoven Septet*

While I was studying and playing in orchestras in Berlin, Germany, I was asked to play in a concert that included the Beethoven Septet for horn, clarinet, bassoon, violin, viola, cello, and double bass. The French horn player was a student of Gerd Seifert, the principal horn of the Berlin Philharmonic. That orchestra was in the top echelon of the world's orchestras, some considered it *the best* orchestra in the world.

For horn players, Gerd Seifert was at the top of the professional ladder. He was instrumental in either making or breaking a horn player's chances in the professional arena. He determined who would play in the annual Richard Wagner Bayreuth Festival which was the crowning achievement for any horn player.

As a teenager, I went to Boston Symphony concerts and sometimes their principal horn player would make obvious mistakes. I thought it was a pity that they didn't have a horn player who was at the same level as the rest of the orchestra. What I did not understand at the time was that playing the horn is precarious. Even the very best players will make mistakes that are obvious to everyone.

In a concert I attended of duets with Itzhak Perlman and Pinchas Zukerman, there were a few instances where I was able to hear Perlman make slight corrections to the notes. These corrections were done so quickly and were so small that it is unlikely that the audience picked up on it at all.

But unlike the violin, where a player can easily and quickly correct so that the audience doesn't even notice, when a horn player misses something, it is blatantly obvious to even the unseasoned listeners.

My theory is that this is why the majority of horn players have a defensive stance. They can be extremely emotional and combative. In an orchestra, it is often the principal horn player who will challenge the conductor in an aggressive way.

When Gerd Seifert walked into our Beethoven Septet rehearsal to give us a coaching, there was a lot of nervousness in the air. Everyone was on edge. His criticisms were harsh, even cruel, and often devastating. It was quite an ordeal. His students later told me that if they could withstand a lesson with Seifert, playing in front of an audience or auditioning committee was a breeze. Nothing was as frightening as playing for Gerd Seifert.

## *Story #3, Clarinetist*

In graduate school, one of my fellow students was a very gifted clarinetist. There was a transcendent quality when he played. You wanted it to just keep going and never stop. His tone, phrasing, musicality, and technique were superb. He did his Carnegie Hall debut during that time, and I was there to drink in the beauty as he played.

Afterwards, I asked him about whether he got nervous and how he handled it. His reply was, "For me, it isn't about who is in the audience or where I am playing. I am always playing for an audience of one."

I didn't quite understand what he meant by this. Did he mean his clarinet teacher, or maybe his wife? Later, when he left to become a Christian missionary, I realized that God was his audience of one. That was who he played for and what mattered to him the most.

===

I include these three very different performance stories to show how **who we think is in the audience makes a big impact** on our experience. Do we see the audience as a scary group that is out to get us or an enthusiastic group of supporters that are delighted to have us perform? It is worthwhile to be totally honest with ourselves and to see what fears we may have about the audience itself.

## REALITY CHECK, THE AUDIENCE

Think about it for a minute. If someone shows up for one of your concerts or recitals, their desire is that it be a pleasing experience. They may or may not have paid money for a ticket, but for sure they have carved out some of their own life to come and sit in the concert hall (they could be doing other things).

**The audience wants you to do well, too.**

They want the concert to be a good return on the investment of their time (which is the only thing any of us truly possesses). Our time is a bank account of the minutes in our lives. Even if someone came out of obligation and not by their own choosing, they still would rather have it be enjoyable.

Watching someone feel devastated is not what they signed up for. They would rather see and hear you do well. So, they want you to do your best, just the same way that you do. They are your allies.

**Even a music critic
would rather hear an inspired performance
than have to sit through someone not doing well.**


## SUPPORTIVE AUDIENCE IMAGE

It is worthwhile to create an image for yourself of a friendly and supportive audience. Even if it is an audition, they are looking for people who can do a good job. They will be happy if you do well.

Before you attempt to create a positive image of the audience, it is important to first **find out what is there in your subconscious.**

=== STRATEGY ===

## Personal Investigation about the Audience

1. Resolve that **you will not make any value judgments** about whether you should or should not feel this or that way.

2. **Write out what you think most of the people in the audience will be thinking as you are playing.** Stream of consciousness, no evaluations. Think of different people who might be there. Make it up. Let your imagination run without restrictions. It can even be funny.

In the same way that there are lots of feelings in our subconscious that come out in dreams, this writing about the audience is a chance to see what your subconscious may have in there about what might happen in your upcoming performance.

If you want to take it even further, you can prompt yourself with questions like, "What would be a terrible audience to have to play for?" or "What would be the best audience to play for?"

3. After writing it all out, **take a break.** Go out for a walk or do something else that will take your focus off what you just wrote.

4. Later, come back to what you have written and this time with your logical mind, **evaluate how true you think those ideas are** (what you wrote).

===

## What Are They Thinking About?

The funny thing is that people tend to think that other people are much more focused on them than the other people really are. While you are playing, people in the audience may be thinking of other things and not really paying attention at all.

Usually, it is only a very few people, maybe your mother or your wife, who will be able to keep their focus on what you are doing for very long. The rest of the people's focus will go in and out, noticing some things and completely missing others. You may have been believing that what you are doing is their primary interest, but it may not be that way at all.

During orchestra auditions, we were sometimes out in the hall eating pizza. We *were* listening, but not in the way that the people auditioning may have thought. So as you read through your projections about what you thought the audience might be thinking, ask yourself, "Is this really true?"

Doing this *Personal Investigation about the Audience* is extremely helpful and gives us a chance to neutralize our worries about being judged or criticized by the audience.

## Byron Katie's "The Work"

An expanded way to work with this is to do one of Byron Katie's *Judge Your Neighbor* worksheets with its primary questions of, "Is it true? Can you absolutely know it's true?

How do you react – what happens – when you believe that thought? Who would you be without that thought?"

There are also turn-arounds that switch the statements the other way. It is fascinating how this inquiry method can neutralize underlying stuck beliefs. There are also YouTube videos of her doing her process with people.

## SUPPORTIVE INDIVIDUALS

Another helpful strategy is to think of one or more individuals who you think are there in the audience supporting you. Play for them. They are on your team. For you, they are the important ones. Like the clarinetist in the story above, having a clear notion of who he was playing for (his concept of God), put him in a mindset where he was unfazed by the audience or the importance of that particular performance.

An added benefit of this is that it restructures the concept of the audience being a big crowd (= you are out numbered) and instead, in your mind it is just individual people. Your *primal brain* will probably do better when you have that image. If you see them as individual *supportive* people, that's even better.

### The Opposite

It's really about finding what works for you as an individual. Whereas for many people, having supportive individuals there rooting for them will make the audience feel more friendly, it might not be that way for you.

A pianist once told me that he never wanted any family members to come to his performances because when he walked out on stage, he wanted to drop his everyday persona and only focus on becoming the music itself. When he was deeply absorbed in the music, he was not the person his family perceived him to be. Having them there in the audience could pull him back into his everyday self, the self he wanted to put aside while he was performing.

It also may be more beneficial for you to have an inner image of the audience being one large mass, without individuals at all.

**Whatever the image is that**

**makes your *primal brain* feel**

**less vulnerable and more in control,**

**it is worthwhile figuring out what that is**

**and then using it.**

## SELF-CRITIC

Looking again at #2 on the list that was suggested above (about what you think the audience will be thinking as you are playing) can also be used to show you what *you, your inner judge,* anticipates thinking about your performance.

This is useful information. In psychology, this is called *projection*. Whatever thoughts and beliefs we carry about ourselves, we will project onto others (and think that is their opinion).

This is especially true with anything we think or feel *but do not want to admit to thinking or feeling*. We project that onto other people and react to them accordingly. Often, these projections turn out to not be true at all.

However, if we have these judgments within ourselves (often picked up from critical parents or teachers in the past) it is better to get those cards out on the table where we have a chance to deal with them.

Once you know what they are, you could use the Byron Katie inquiry questions or use hypnosis to reprogram yourself. For additional effective methods, keep an eye out for my upcoming book, *Clear & Free of Unwanted Thoughts & Emotions*.

## HEALTHY GOALS vs UNREACHABLE STANDARDS

Another helpful investigation is to see if you are out of alignment with the reality of your playing level (and therefore setting unreachable standards for yourself).

For example, let's imagine the various levels of expertise are categorized in numbers, 1-50, with 50 being the most advanced soloist. If you have the idea that you are at level 15, and you find yourself playing in a way that is *not* a level 15, you could be all upset. You might berate yourself and say, "That was bad!"

But what is really going on is that you had a false idea of your own level of expertise. The reality is that your playing is a level 12. You are doing just fine at level 12. By pretending to yourself that you are at 15, you are just setting yourself up to fail.

My students sometimes say they are nervous to play for me. Why? I love my students and only want to help them realize their musical goals. I am not going to be hard on them. Of course, we always want other people to think well of us, but there is really nothing to fear here. So what is it that makes them worried?

What the students are probably actually nervous about is that when they play, **it will show that they are not at *the level they want to think they are.*** Because there was a time at home that it worked so well, they have the idea that this should now be their new skill level. Or maybe they think that I think they should be at a higher skill level (projection).

Either way, if they don't play very well in the lesson, the reality is that the way it went at home is not their skill level yet. That new skill level is not yet solidified (see Chapter 3-4).

The good news is, that if they could do it once at home, they are well on their way to getting there. It's just that they won't fully arrive there until it becomes solidified.

So rather than berating yourself if it doesn't go as well as you would like, it is possible to just see anything that happens as information about what still needs to be solidified. It all takes practice. We musicians certainly know that! Think of a child who is learning to walk. They will lose their balance for a while and will fall down a lot. That is not a horrible defeat. That is just the level of expertise they have at that point.

It is the same for each of us. We are where we are.

The healthy attitude is then to set our sites on goals of where we would like to be, and do our best to work our way up to that. We are not *wrong or bad* along the way. We are all works in progress, even the musicians who are at the top.

### Story: The Winning Basketball Coach

A winning basketball coach was asked about how he was able to switch teams and still have whichever team he was coaching win the championship.

His secret? For each player there were particular skills he was helping them improve. He worked with the players individually, always encouraging and pushing them to better their own skills and contributions to the team.

He never compared them to the competition and never even talked about winning a game. What he was striving for was that the players each play at their greatest potential. That is where he put the focus. And he got results!

===

**Only compare yourself to your own best self.**

You are not going out on stage to be Itzhak Perlman or Hilary Hahn. Your job is to be you. The person to measure yourself against is *your own self functioning at your full potential.*

You are where you are today. Next year things will be different. The goal is play in the way that you are capable of today.

# DEALING WITH THE FEAR ITSELF

## ALLOWING THE FEAR

During my music studies, I remember noticing that the people who got nervous before a recital played better during their recitals than the people who said they weren't nervous ahead of time. I experimented with different ways to handle my own nervousness when it came up.

*EXAMPLE: A recital or end of semester jury is coming up and I feel nervous.*

Here are two options:

**Option 1.** Each time I feel the fear come up, I do my best to calm myself. I tell myself that it will all be alright. Nothing to fear... Then **I distract myself** by putting my attention on doing something that keeps me focused on that task.

**Option 2.** Each time the fear comes up, **I sit down and just watch myself** as it happens without trying to push it down or rationalize it away. I notice how my physical body feels. I watch to see what happens with my breath. As I am doing this, I also know that I am ok. "I am sitting here having an experience of feeling fearful."

You may want to try both ways of handling it. What I discovered was that for me, option #2 was *a lot* better. With option #1, it was sort of like saving up all that nervous energy. Then as I walked out on stage it would all be there. With option #2, I felt more powerful. I could handle having the feelings. I didn't die. It didn't last forever. I was OK.

**On the day of the recital or concert**, when the nervous feelings came up, I welcomed them because what I discovered was that **I could not *stay that nervous* for very long.** If I let it happen first, I was in a better place by the time I started the performance.

## BREATHING TECHNIQUES, Getting Control

### === STRATEGY ===

## Controlling Your Breath as a Way to Calm Yourself

When we feel anxious, we tend to breathe more rapidly and with shallow breathing. A good way to counteract this tendency is to breathe slowly and deeply, filling your diaphragm (not just your lungs/chest). It helps to clear your lungs as much as possible first. Blow out as far as you can or sing a long note until there is absolutely no breath left. Then try one of the breathing patterns below.

*These were also included in Chapter 6.*

**1. Counting** is the most common technique, but there are many variations of that. You can try different ones and see what works out the best for you.

IN-2-3-4, rest, rest, OUT-2-3-4, IN-2-3-4… (the rests are waiting)
or
IN-2-3-4, OUT-2-3-4, rest, rest, IN-2-3-4…

2. As above with the IN through your nose and OUT through your mouth, like gently blowing out a candle.

4. Breathe IN with eyes closed, OUT with eyes open, releasing any busy thoughts.

5. Put your attention on the sensations as the air comes in and out of your body while breathing normally (without attempting to change it in any way).

6. Alternate nostril breathing. Block one nostril, breathe out and in through the other nostril, then switch.

# STEP BY STEP: OVERCOMING FEAR

The *primal brain* thinks in symbolic images, so changing our inner image of the audience will be a big benefit in subduing the fear reaction of the primal brain when we stand in front of a group.

**But how does that part of our brain learn?** This is not the part of the brain we use to memorize the state capitols for a geography test at school. This part of us is all about **action**, what actually happened?

Training this part of the brain is like training an animal. If you have ever trained a pet, you can use what you learned by doing that to help with training yourself to perform with greater comfort. With your pet, you probably found out that the best method is to:

- work step-by-step
- do lots of repetition
- use praise, positive reinforcement for correct actions

## *Story: Scared to Dive*

Where I grew up, there weren't any swimming pools where we could go in the summer. All the neighborhood families belonged to a place where there was a small lake that was good for swimming. The owners brought in a lot of beach sand to make it nicer and put up a raft on barrels that people could swim out to for diving.

When I was seven years old, we spent the summer at a university with a large pool. I was doing well with learning to swim and even was able to dive off the big diving board into the deep pool.

The summer I was eight, we were back home. There was a day camp that used the same small lake for swimming and boating activities. On the first day, while in the changing room for swimming, I heard some older girls talking about how easy it is to drown. There was also talk about water moccasins (a water snake) living in that lake. They said people had seen those snakes from the raft.

I knew that there were eels in the lake. I had seen them before, but the water moccasin snakes were supposed to be very dangerous.

When we got down to the lake, I swam successfully out to the raft and climbed the ladder up onto it. I began to feel afraid about diving. I spent the rest of swim-time standing around on the raft and at the end, dove off and swam quickly back to shore.

The next day when I got out to the raft I was too scared to dive at all. Instead, when swim-time was over, I held my nose to jump off and swam back.

The third day it was worse. I was unable to dive or even jump into the water. I made my way down the ladder and swam back.

This time I told my mother when I got home what was going on. She was a lifesaver. She called the people at the camp and got permission to go back in the early evening when no one else was there. I swam to the raft and she (being an adult) was able to just walk out to it. The water was well below her neck.

Filled with fear, I crouched down on the edge of the raft. There was my mom standing in front of me with her arms open telling me to just jump down into her arms. It was so hard. I was just SO scared. Finally, I inched off the raft and into her waiting arms.

We did it again and again. Each time I was less afraid. Soon I could jump off again. Again and again. Finally, I was able to DIVE off. After doing that a number of times, we left. How lucky I am that my mom did that for me.

The funny part: What I was only told later was that while my mother was standing in front of the raft holding her arms out reassuringly to me and saying it would all be safe and ok, there was a fish swimming between her legs and even sucking a bit on one of her legs. We have laughed about what would have happened if she had screamed. They would have needed a boat to get me back to shore! My mom was a hero. Thank you, Mom.

I include this story here because it describes so well what is often needed to change a fear pattern that is coming from our *primal brain*. It is often not reasonable at all, so just reasoning it out probably will not make the difference.

The change needs to be an action. To this part of our brains, **actions are reality**. When we are able to do an action that belies our previous fear, that shows our *primal brain* that this is real. We CAN do this. It IS ok.

# CHANGING A FEAR PATTERN.
# What CAN you do? Start there.

The first step is to figure something that you *can* do. Then reinforce that with repetition. Congratulate yourself each time. Then when you feel ready, create a next step that is just a bit more challenging and takes you in the direction of your goal.

### === STRATEGY ===
## Building Up from Where You Are

EXAMPLE: *Charlotte is petrified at the idea of having anyone else hear her play the fiddle. She lives alone in a place with only distant neighbors (so no one hears her play at home). She would like to be able to play in a local fiddle group that plays at different events near where she lives. Let's assume she is at a level where she can easily play their music from memory.*

1. Evaluate. What can she already do?
*When Charlotte is home, she can already play all the music the group plays.*

2. Solidify the level of skill she already has.
*Charlotte chooses one fiddle tune that is particularly easy to play and goes through some of the methods laid out in Chapters 3 and 4.*

3. Create an easy challenge. Something that moves in the direction of where she would like to go, but is still within an easy range.
*Charlotte has a mobile phone with a record app on it. She records herself playing the fiddle tune. Then she listens to it and congratulates herself on how good it sounds.*

4. Make it a bit more difficult.
*Next, Charlotte decides to make a video with her phone. She puts on the kind of clothes the fiddlers wear when they perform and she makes a video (just for herself) while she plays the fiddle tune. She didn't like how it came out at first, but after repeated tries, she got a video she felt good about.*

5. More risky.
*Charlotte creates a YouTube channel. She uploads her video with the private setting so that only she can view it. As she watches, she congratulates herself on how it looks and sounds. It's not a professional video, but then again, she isn't a*

*professional fiddler either. It is just nice to see that she can do it.*

6. Even more.
*Next, Charlotte changes the YouTube video setting so that if a person has the exact link, they will be able to view it. She sends the link to a few people that she trusts. It is a BIG step, but by now she is ready. She can see how many views there are and that is scary, but it also feels empowering.*

I think you get the idea. The next step is to make the video public. Then she can send a link to the leader of the fiddle group as a sort of audition. Soon she will be a valuable member of the local fiddle group.

## Making A YouTube Video

In the last chapter (#7) there was a section about the value of doing videos as a performance preparation and to help with improving your technique (also see Chapter 4, Step #5).

As was described in the example above, making a video can also help with overcoming the fear of performing. If you set the goal of making a video that is good enough to upload to YouTube, any performing anxieties you may have will likely come up to a certain extent with just the video challenge. This gives you a chance to work them through on a smaller scale.

## Rehearsing in Small Time to prepare for the Big Time

See *Playing In Front of a Practice Audience*, Chapter 7. This is definitely an important step in convincing your *primal brain* that you can function well in front of an audience.

Also, going through all the distraction challenges in Chapter 4 gives you a tremendous advantage when your concert date comes up. That way, you will have already withstood many difficulties – like playing with bright lights shining in your eyes. As you walk out on stage, you are then prepared to handle any new circumstances you may face.

## Do a lot of performing

Part of what can make performing difficult is that a person can experience something like a mild form of shock. It's a brand-new experience; you don't know what will happen. But **if we perform repeatedly, the newness and shock wear off.** We cannot stay on such high alert for very long. In the same way that playing a particular passage 100 times gives us greater ease with it, the more we perform, the more **we can anticipate the experiences and the results our body's inner pharmacy may bring about**.

So the good news is that the more we perform, the better we get at knowing how to focus and handle our energy when we are on stage.

**An Added Note:** Once you go through all the trouble of getting a piece or whole program up to a level that you can perform it, why not get as much mileage out of it as possible? Play the same program in as many venues as possible. I did this for my Masters Recital. I played the same program in five different places during a two-month period.

The well-known soloists that perform with various orchestras often play the same concerto repeatedly for years.

# OTHER WAYS TO DEAL WITH FEAR

## Hypnosis Recordings

Hypnosis recordings are available for accelerated learning and improved performance. Choose one that does not have background music. The saccharine music on a lot of these recordings often does not work for those of us who are musicians ourselves. Getting a recording without background music also means you have the option to play your own choice of music in the background (on another device). Search for *hypnosis for musicians* or something similar.

## Beta Blockers

You may or may not know that many performing musicians use drugs called *beta blockers*. These drugs are designed to treat hypertension and angina. They somehow are able to keep our hearts from beating too fast and our muscles from going into the push-pull that creates trembling.

### *Story: Brahms Quintet*

One of my musician friends kept telling me how wonderfully the beta blockers worked for him when he was performing. He gave me some to use for an upcoming orchestra audition. The effect was quite impressive. When I felt nervous, I often was bothered by tension in my bow arm that created a bit of "bouncing bow" on long slow notes. But with the beta blocker, my bow arm was like silk! No difficulties with controlling my bow at all. Unfortunately, I still didn't get the job (that was the same audition my hair fell down, Chapter 9), but I was impressed with how the drug had worked.

I also noticed that it seemed to take the excitement out of the event. I decided that for performing in concerts and recitals it would not be a good thing for me. I needed that extra energy to really project an experience to the audience while I played. I wanted the music to penetrate their very being, not be lovely but emotionally flat.

This was well illustrated when I played viola in the Brahms Quintet as part of a summer music festival. The two violinists and the cellist were all taking beta blockers. The pianist and I were not. I was very "on" for that performance. I loved the music and the pianist was someone whose musicality and expertise I greatly admired. The violinists and cellist were colleagues I often played with and that I had a good feeling about, too. The performance went very well.

Afterwards, at the meet-the-musicians, people were delighted with my performance. What particularly struck me was one person's comment that, "You and the pianist were on fire! I didn't feel anything from the other three, but you two made the whole thing come alive."

===

## KNOW THAT FEAR DOES NOT NEED TO STOP YOU, Having Courage

It is not just when performing music that we need to be able to *continue even when we feel worried about how things may go*. Courage is an excellent attribute to possess in all kinds of situations.

Knowing through our own personal experience that fear does not need to stop us from doing what we want to do, or doing what is needed, is one of the great gifts of learning to perform music. We learn how to be courageous when situations get tough and the pressure is on.

### *Story: Playing Through Her Fear*

Lisa took violin lessons with me from the time she was in 6th grade until she graduated from high school. When she started, she was moving into that age when most people feel pretty insecure. For a young teenager to get up in front of an audience and do something brand new that she wasn't very good at yet was a real challenge. Helping Lisa to be able to perform with confidence was going to be an important part of our lessons.

Lisa was smart and had a terrific personality. She was not rebellious or contrary, but listened well and did her best to follow my directions and suggestions.

I really wanted her to have a good experience with performing, so I did my best to set things up so that we would have the greatest chance of success.

For her first recital, we chose a piece that would be very easy for her. I also suggested that I play along with her in the performance. That way she would not be alone on the stage, would not need to be stressed about the difficulty of the notes, and if she missed something I would keep playing and she could just get back in.

We worked on solidifying her piece, and I told her repeatedly that our goal was that we go out on the stage and play through the piece. It was not important if she made mistakes. If she just was able to get through it, that would be enough to call it a success.

First recital: Lisa did it. She played her piece, even though she was visibly shaking all over. There were mistakes, but SHE DID IT. She did not let fear stop her.

Next recital: It was a bit better. She was still nervous, made some minor mistakes, but GOT THROUGH IT AGAIN and was not shaking so visibly anymore.

Next recital: Even better. And on it went through the years.

When Lisa turned 16 she was nervous about taking her drivers' test, but we talked about it, and I reminded her that she had now learned to do something even if she was feeling fear.

She passed her drivers' test the first time.

When Lisa graduated from high school she was the valedictorian of her class. To this day, on the wall in the studio, I have a newspaper clipping of her wearing her graduation cap and gown, standing at the podium and addressing the whole town on behalf of her class. Bravo!

===

This is one example of how overcoming a fear of playing music in public also teaches us skills that will come to our aid again and again as we navigate through the challenges, triumphs, twists and turns of our lives.

## CHAPTER NINE

# Where Will You Perform?

Where will you be performing?
1. AUDITIONING
2. CONCERTS & RECITALS
3. MAINTAINING FOCUS & ENDURANCE
4. PERFORMING IS A PACKAGE
- Performance Routine
- Bowing to the Audience
- Warming Up Before You Perform
- Clothing

There is always more we could do to improve our overall technique, but having an upcoming performance is an opportunity to set clear goals, and finish something with a feeling of accomplishment and closure.

Knowing the performance date gives us a timeframe. It helps us pace how we work on a piece, organize our practice time and, if necessary, it can inspire us to give it an extra push when the time is getting close.

The pieces we choose to perform also divide our music studies into sections, and can inspire us to develop the techniques which are needed to perform particular pieces.

## Where Will You Be Performing?

The type of performing we will be doing makes a big difference in choosing the best ways to prepare for it. At best, we want to use our time and energy to produce the optimal results. Preparing for an orchestral audition will be different than preparing to give a solo recital or do a studio recording.

### Story: *Wildly Popular for just one night*

I played some backup parts on an album for a singing duo. They invited me to come and play at a nightclub where they were doing their album-release party. After singing a few songs without me, they called me up on the stage to play with them.

The crowd went wild, cheering enthusiastically, even stumping their feet. I was a star!

I had to laugh to myself at the irony of it. All I did was play some long slow notes as backup. In the orchestra, I often had to play difficult solos, and I had never gotten even half that amount of enthusiasm!

===

# AUDITIONING

Unlike a concert or recital, an audition is a test. You will pass or fail and often be given a numerical rank. In this case they will deduct points for any deviation from what is written in the music or what it says in the rules.

As a principal player in the orchestra, I judged many auditions for the orchestra. I was also an adjudicator for high school students. Below is what I learned as a result of being on both sides – the judge and the one being judged.

## Follow the Rules

Of course, you want to play all the correct rhythms and notes with good intonation, the correct dynamics, good phrasing and good tone. But for an audition the focus also needs to be on **following directions.** What is it they are looking for?

If it is a high school all-state audition, and they want 3-octave scales in a particular rhythm at a particular metronome speed, do it just the way they have specified.

Get the correct edition of the auditioning piece and follow the fingerings and bowings in that edition. Photocopies are only acceptable to avoid page turns.

Listen to recordings and find out what the accepted tempo for the required audition piece is. Don't play it faster or slower.

## Your Goal Is Accuracy

Although they would like you to play musically and with expression, your primary focus should be ACCURACY.

## Be Respectful, Have A Likeable Personality

Another important aspect of auditioning well is to be respectful. Whether it is an all-state judge, a college end-of-semester jury, or an orchestral auditioning committee, these people are judges.

They want to be treated with respect.

People are influenced by a person's physical appearance. If you show up for an all-state audition with ratty jeans, your friends may think you look cool, but the judges probably will not. The judges will take much more kindly to you, if they feel you are taking this seriously and are **cooperative and diligent**.

## SCHOLARSHIPS and END OF SEMESTER COLLEGE JURIES (music students)

For college juries, scholarship auditions, college admittance auditions, or graduate school auditions, project an image of someone who is serious about playing their game (whatever that is), as well as playing your instrument well.

Students who come across as contrary, arrogant, self-absorbed or disrespectful in any way, are not winning any points here, and are losing them for sure.

## ORCHESTRA AUDITIONS

## For orchestra playing the priorities are as follows:

#1 is Rhythm

#2 is Intonation (notes in tune)

#3 is Musicality, including playing in a way that is stylistically correct for each era and composer

#4 for string players is Tone (sound quality), unless the audition is for principal (1st chair)

**Important:**

Be sure to make the rests the correct length.

Careful not to rush rapid passages of fast notes. **That is a big no-no!**

Many people auditioning spend more time preparing their solo piece than the orchestral excerpts. That is a big mistake. **The auditioning committee wants to know what you will contribute to the orchestra.**

The notes may be easier in Mozart, but that is also where your weaknesses can be most obvious, especially keeping a steady tempo. Prepare the Mozart excerpt extremely carefully, with the metronome.

## Dress Well

Even if you will be playing an orchestral audition behind a screen, dress well. The orchestra manager, or whoever is working with the people who are auditioning, should also see you as **a respectful team player.** If you get the job, you will want to have a good relationship with that person.

Your clothing should also be comfortable enough to play in without difficulty. I made the mistake of putting my hair up for an orchestra audition. At that time in Germany, the auditions were not behind a screen. As I was playing my concerto audition-piece, my hair began to gradually fall out and come down. It was very distracting to me, and probably also to those on the committee that were watching (I did not get the job).

## *Story: His Personality Disqualified Him*

A violinist once told me that she went to audition for an orchestra and was taken aback when she heard another violinist warming up in the room next door.

What she heard was an exquisite sound, flawless technique, playing at a standard much higher than her own. Should she just go home? She went ahead and did the audition, even though she didn't think she would get the job. She wasn't hired, but neither was the violinist next door. Why?

It turned out he came from the New York Philharmonic and had been fired because of his difficult personality. His reputation preceded him, and he could not even get a job in a part-time orchestra.

**Orchestras want team players**, not "bad apples that will ruin the bunch." If you are auditioning for an orchestra job, put yourself in the mindset of **doing your part to benefit the group.**

# CONCERTS & RECITALS
## *Make It Your Gift to The Audience*

The people in the audience want to have a pleasant experience. They may be music lovers, people who care about you, or people who were obligated to attend for some reason. All of them are giving you some of their time.

**Giving someone our time and focus is giving someone part of our lives.** We each have a limited number of minutes within which to experience life. If someone gives you their time and focus, make it worthwhile for them.

**Let your desire be to give something back to those people listening.** Play for *them*, not for yourself. All those many hours of practicing can be for you, but when you walk out on the stage, **play for the people who are listening**. It is not about you. It is about them. Be generous in your focus and desire.

Most people in the audience would much prefer to have an experience that touches them or lifts their spirits than hear someone play all the correct notes in a boring way. Make it as beautiful as you can, let the notes sing, put some heart and soul into it if you can.

Remember, they would much rather you create a wonderful experience for them, than watch you get all involved in your own self-judgment. **This is not a test. It is a chance to give something of yourself to others.**

## PERFORMING IS A PACKAGE:
### *It is Not Just Playing the Music*

A common mistake is for people to only practice the actual piece of music that they will perform, forgetting that the performance is a total package. Pity if he walks out awkwardly, doesn't know how to bow (more awkwardness), gets flustered putting his music out, isn't clear about how to start the piece… It can begin to look like a comedy routine. The audience doesn't want to be empathizing with all a performer's awkwardness.

All those little things (bowing to the audience, etc.) are so much easier to learn than playing your instrument. Don't let them detract from all that you have worked so hard to achieve. When you are comfortable and confident, the audience will be more relaxed, too, and they will enjoy it more.

Take some time to feel secure with all the elements that go along with performing your piece.

### PERFORMANCE ROUTINE

Elements to include in your performances:

1. Before walking out on stage affirm to yourself what you goal is.

2. Walk out.

3. It is nice to smile at someone you like in the audience.

4. Bow towards the audience, look down and count 1-10 (see BOWING below).

5. Put your music on the stand, if you are using music. *Note that this is after the bow.*

6. Think of how your piece will sound, so you know what you are doing before you start.

7. PLAY.

8. Often it is good to freeze for just a moment when you finish playing. Imagine there are extra beats of rest at the end of the piece.

9. Feet together.

10. Bow toward the audience.

11. Acknowledge your accompanist, if you did not bow together.

12. Collect your music.

13. Walk off.

14. Congratulate yourself. This is a way to create a positive imprint in your subconscious about performing.

**All of these elements are part of your performance.**

## BOWING Before and After Your Performance

- Bring your feet together first. Bowing with your feet spread apart looks pretty amusing.

- If you are a string player, let the tip of your bow point downward or up in the air, not at the audience.

- It is nice to smile at the audience just before you bow.

- Lean over, look down at your shoes, and count to ten.

You are doing the audience a favor by just **bowing in a normal natural way.** A strange or awkward bow may make more of an impression than the music itself.

## WARMING UP Before You Perform

Each performer figures out what is the best way for them to be ready to perform. You definitely need to arrive at the hall in enough time for your instrument to acclimate to the hall temperature and humidity. You also need to get your muscles ready to go and your mind focused.

One thing that seems to be pretty universal is that this preparation time is usually getting everything all "well oiled" and well organized. This is not the time for a passionate rendition of the music you will play. Instead most people will focus on scales, arpeggios and other warm-ups they do at the beginning of their daily practice sessions. Instilling a sense of competent calmness is a good way to prepare.

If there is a particular passage that is tricky, people will often "set this up" by playing it slowly, precisely, and calmly. It is a sort of "getting your ducks in a row" approach.

Each person will find what works best for them, but taking time to really evaluate what is the best approach for you, is time well spent.

## CLOTHING: It Makes a Difference

Wear clothing that:

- does not distract from the music itself
- is well suited to the type of event/venue/gig
- will be comfortable for you to perform in

You have probably been to a concert where the performer wore something that got so much attention that it was all people talked about afterwards. The best performers know what sort of clothing will *enhance* the overall experience for the audience but not detract from the enjoyment of the music itself.

We had a situation in my Connecticut orchestra where the orchestra manager put it into our contracts that "all women must wear black hose/stockings under long black dresses/skirts/formal slacks." The orchestra depended on wealthy donors and some of them complained that they were seeing bare ankles on the stage. They evidently did not want to support players who did not appear to take their jobs seriously enough to dress the part. It may seem silly, but these are the realities in the professional musician's world.

During my years of playing for high-society weddings and functions in the Newport, Rhode Island mansions, I often thought the way we were dressed was more important to the people who hired us than how well we played the music. For these high-society functions, appearances were their top priority – both the organizers and the guests.

> **Be sure you are comfortable playing
> in whatever you will wear.**

As mentioned before, I had a musician friend in Berlin who used to ride the subways wearing his concert clothes (bow tie, cummerbund, and tails) just so that he would begin to feel "normal" dressed that way. It helped him to be more relaxed when he was performing in the same clothing.

## Interviews with Classical Musicians

The "Living the Classical Life" Series has many interesting interviews with some of today's top performers in the Classical musicians' world. You can listen to what they have to say about performing and what it has been like for them. The interviews are on both YouTube and Vimeo.

# CHAPTER TEN

# *The Basics*

What's the story of a musical composition?
Short answer: I was home.
  I went somewhere else, then came back home.
Melodic answer: do – re or ti – do.
Harmonic answer: Tonic – Dominant – Tonic.

This book is about performing at your best. What's the one-sentence version?
Answer: **Give yourself the gift of preparing thoroughly.**

Both *getting the big picture* and *going deep into a subject* are important for really absorbing any body of information. In the previous chapters there has been quite a bit of detail. For this final chapter we'll look at things from a pared-down, simple perspective.

Below is a short summary of each of the chapters. I hope this will be a good way for you to integrate what's been discussed here. A quick review can be a good way to help with digesting what has been gained.

## Chapter 1: Having a Clear *Sound Idea*

Basic concept: We need to know **what it is we are trying to play.** If we don't have that, what is it we are doing? Figuring out *how the music goes* and *how we would like it to sound* are essential.

## Chapter 2: Embody the Feeling

Creating a *body feeling image* of what it feels like to play the piece with confidence, solidity, and ease. Use practice strategies that teach your body to do what you want it to. Also experiment with what visualizing the muscle movements can do for you.

## Chapter 3: Making It Reliable

Repetition is, of course, the most essential part of this. Giving it time to digest is also important.

**Phases of Preparing a Piece for Performance:**

1. Learning how the piece goes, creating your ***sound idea.*** You know how it goes and how you want to be able to play it.

2. Working on the piece enough that **you can play all the sections at the tempo** you would like to perform it.

3. Making it **reliable**. This involves playing it repeatedly. Getting it to the point that you can play it multiple times in a row without mistakes.

4. **Giving it time to digest**. Different parts of our brains record memory in different ways. It takes time for an *imprint of competence* to transfer from one part of the brain to another. Once it does, our playing of that piece becomes more reliable.

5. Being able to **play the piece under pressure**, when conditions are not ideal or when things are challenging.

6. Being able to play through the **entire program twice in a row** in a way that you feel good about. This develops your stamina (both physically and mentally).

## Chapter 4: Making It Solid Under Pressure

It's not just being able to play it reliably when all the conditions are familiar. Solidifying it means challenging yourself to be able to play your piece under difficult circumstances. Suggestions included a number of ways to make it harder to play – distractions, different clothing, lighting, locations, surprising sounds, people too close, etc.

## Chapter 5: When Mistakes Happen

Developing the ability to stay focused and keep going when you make mistakes.

## Chapter 6: Memorizing Your Music

In order to have an intimate relationship with the music, we need to be familiar enough with it that *we remember it*.

Three basic ways to remember your piece, plus Association:

- Auditory Memory (how it sounds)
- Visual Memory (how the notes look and where you are on the page)
- Muscle Memory (what your body is doing when you are playing the music)
- Using Association (connecting it to other things you know)

A combination of these ways to remember gives us the most solid memory of the piece.

The 1,000 repetitions of Dr. Suzuki make it clear that if you think you aren't good at remembering, it is probably that you simply have not done the number of repetitions needed to teach yourself *how* to remember something. Keep at it. Don't give up. Remember that ALL the children were able to learn the haiku after 1,000 repetitions.

## Chapter 7: Performance Nerves

Fear #1: Fear of Failure. Doing the strategies in Chapters 1-6 will help you feel so confident of your piece that you are unlikely to think you might fail.

However, there are more strategies that can help with the extra nervous energy that most people experience when they perform in front of an audience. Learning to function with the added energy is a skill in itself. One strategy is to get your heart pumping rapidly and then play. Making recordings and videos are a big help, as they put the pressure on, but in a less intense way.

Playing in front of practice audiences is extremely helpful.

**Chapter 8: Stage Fright**

Fear #2: Fear of Attack/Criticism/Judgment. This is more intense than just being nervous. This comes from the primal fear of being attacked.

Dealing with this needs to involve what I call your *primal brain*. This part of us functions in the same way as in other animals. The *primal brain's* key agenda is keeping us alive. That means staying safe and getting what we need.

To deal with the *primal brain,* we need to communicate in the ways that it understands – symbolic imagery and action. Defining who our audience is (allies or enemies), running a reality check on our subconscious beliefs – about the audience and our own self-critic – and strategies to deal with the fear-experience itself were covered here.

This chapter also included how hypnosis helps us understand the subconscious, using beta blockers, and the importance of developing the courage that comes from knowing that fear does not need to stop us.

**Chapter 9: Where are You Going to Perform?**

If you are doing an audition, it is important to consider what the judges are looking for and do your best to fulfill that. Accuracy, and a team-player personality are important for the orchestra. Highschool adjudications demand following the criteria exactly (which edition of the music, how the scales are to be played, tempos, etc.).

Solo recitals are your chance to give a gift to the audience. Make it a worthwhile experience for them. They are more interested in how the music makes them feel than if you miss a few notes.

Learning the basic performance routine is a favor to everyone – the audience and yourself. Just learn to do it in a normal, graceful way and save the excitement for the music itself. Dressing appropriately is important for any performance.

**Chapter 10: In Conclusion**

A brief review of what was covered in this book.

I hope you have enjoyed this book and that it will help to bring out the marvelous performer that you are. There are lots of audiences just waiting to appreciate your musical gifts.

If you enjoyed this book and found it useful, please share it with your friends, and of course, it is always wonderful when someone writes a complimentary review!

Thank you, if you choose to do so!

===

There is a **BONUS CHAPTER** for you
at the end of this book
from
*Success with the Violin and Life*

===

# About the Author

For more than 30 years, Ruth Shilling, M.M. (Viola Performance), taught violin, viola, *String Methods*, and chamber music at the University of Connecticut and UConn CSA. During that time she piloted the Violin for Adults program for adult beginners, which matured into an active chamber music program. Now retired, she offers online "Fix-that-Spot" lessons for violinists and violists. See more about those lessons at violinsuccess.com.

Ruth spent five years studying in Germany with Eberhard Klemmstein, previously of the Reger String Quartet and later the Director of the Erlanger Musikinstitut. During her time in Germany, Ruth played with the RIAS (Radio in the American Sector) Jugend Orchester, The Berliner Bach Gesellschaft, and the Berliner Barock Orchester; and made recordings with both RIAS and the Winsbacher Knabenchor.

## ABOUT THE AUTHOR

In the USA Ruth was the principal violist of New London, Connecticut's Eastern Connecticut Symphony Orchestra, performing and recording with them for 17 years. During that time, she was also a member of the Hop River Chamber Players, the Trillium Trio, and the Minoan Quartet. Ruth resigned from the ECSO after creating the ***All One World Egypt Tours*** business which has now taken her to Egypt more than 50 times.

Ruth Shilling and her Students

Additional recordings with Ruth Shilling (playing viola):
- *So Strong* with Justina & Joyce
- *Awake, Arise, Ascend* with Connie Stardancer, Richard Shulman
- *Keeper of the Holy Grail* with Richard Shulman

See all Ruth's activities: ruthshilling.com
Facebook.com/ruthshillingmm
***Violin Success Series***: violinsuccess.com
Facebook.com/successviolin

# More Books by Ruth Shilling

- Accessing Clear Guidance: Help and Answers Through Inspired Writing & Inner Knowing
- Clear & Free of Unwanted Thoughts & Emotions: 25 Effective Methods

*Violin Success Series*
- SUCCESS with the Violin & Life: Strategies, Techniques, and Tips for Learning Quickly and Doing Well, Vol.1
- Performing at Your Best: A Musician's Guide to Successful Performances, Vol. 2

*Through A Medium's Eyes Series*
*About Life, Love, Mediumship, and the Spirit World*
- Rev. B. Anne Gehman, Vol. 1 (also in LARGE PRINT)
- Carol Gasber, Vol. 2
- Neal Rzepkowski, M.D., Vol. 3

*Books about Egypt*
- The Tomb of Queen Nefertari: Egyptian Gods & Goddesses of the New Kingdom
- Pictures of Ancient Egyptian Gods & Goddesses: Edited Photos
- Egyptian Gods & Goddesses Notebooks with Blank Papyrus-Imprint Pages, Vol. 1-16. Isis, Sekhmet, Horus, Ra, Anubis, Osiris, & more
- SINAI: The Desert & Bedouins of South Sinai's Central Regions. Photos and text by Ruth Shilling.
- Time & Space in the Temples & Pyramids: Egypt Tour

*Adult Coloring Books*
- Marvelous Manifestation Mandalas, Vol. 1
- Magnetic Manifestation Mandalas, Vol. 2
- Miraculous Manifestation Mandalas, Vol. 3
- Angelic Manifestation Mandalas, Vol. 4.

# SUCCESS with the Violin and Life
# BONUS CHAPTER

## CHAPTER ONE

## Practice Being Successful

Skills cannot be bought or given away. We acquire them through our own actions over time. But good guidance and the knowledge of *how to most easily acquire a skill* makes a huge difference. Applying some universal principles for successful achievement can save us vast amounts of time and effort!

Many highly competent people at the top of their fields, including the majority of entrepreneurs, learned to play an instrument when they were young. They invested time and effort in hours of practice, they got a taste for the momentum brought by inspired action and focused desire, and they delighted in the sweet satisfaction of accomplishment.

A man, who made a profession of showing others how to achieve skills in the shortest amount of time, demonstrated one of his strategies in a dramatic way.

### *Story: Success Breeds Success*

John* had never fired a gun in his life and knew nothing about target shooting. He went to a shooting club and asked how long it usually took to achieve a certain level of success. The answer was about 2-3 months.

[ *All of the stories in this book are from the author's own personal experiences, however, many of the names used in the stories have been changed. ]

John first needed to learn how to shoot a pistol. When he fired it the first time there was a kick back and all the guys were laughing at his reaction.

The next thing he did was to walk all the way up to the target, stick the gun right on the bullseye and fire. SUCCESS! Bullseye!

The guys standing around were not impressed. Of course he could get a bullseye if he stuck the gun right on it.

What John then began to do was to gradually move away from the target, constantly shooting directly into the bullseye and each time feeling the satisfaction of achieving his goal.

So his pattern was: **Success, Rejoice, Satisfaction.**

And what was the result? Within *just two weeks* he was shooting at a level that would normally take *2-3 months*.

===

## Practicing Being Successful vs. Using Willpower to Continue While Failing

Why does repeatedly being successful yield better and faster results than trying again and again, despite failing, until you finally get it?

Let's look at the target shooting example.

John's goal may have been to shoot a bullseye at 30 feet. He could have started standing 30 feet away and shooting. Each time he would have failed, but he may have gotten closer and closer with repeated attempts. If he had the willpower to keep trying despite his constant defeats, he would probably eventually be able to achieve his goal. But during that process he would be constantly dealing with defeat.

People who work to achieve skills learn to deal with defeat and keep going, but getting back up on the horse after falling takes effort. It is hard on the ego to fail and we have to use willpower to override feeling deflated by it. Having willpower is good, but constantly dealing with defeat is like pushing uphill rather than coasting downhill.

John, on the other hand, chose to constantly experience being successful. That feeling of "Hurray!" was like the wind at his back. It provided a momentum that naturally wanted to carry him forward.

## Body memory imprint

Another aspect of working with repeated success, as opposed to repeated failures, is that the body learns by doing. If the body does something well or not well, either way it is establishing a sort of groove, like a rut in a field where people keep driving the same route.

Our bodies remember the way it was done before and are most likely to do it in a similar way the next time. It will always be easier to do it that way, rather than a different way.

So if you fail the first time, the next time you attempt to do it, your body will most likely do it in a similar way, which will mean failing again.

If on the other hand, you experience success the first time you try to do something, that makes an imprint in your body memory which will make it more likely that next time you will also be successful.

## Imprint of connection

In the target shooting example John's body, mind and spirit were repeatedly making a connection with the bullseye. This imprint of connection guided him towards replicating that success as he challenged himself to achieve the more difficult goal of moving farther away from the target.

## Visualizing success

Another aspect which contributes to this is the ability to visualize success. Athletes and high achievers are well aware of how the power of visualizing helps them to accomplish their goals. Having a series of successful experiences to draw on helps us to recreate them in our mind's eye.

It is a lot easier to visualize success when we have already experienced it!

## Where does willpower come in?

Willpower always has an important role in learning skills. Without it we would be unfocused and our attempts to achieve things would be short-lived. Even when we are working with the success model, we will have defeats. We will still need to "get back on the horse" when we don't achieve our goals.

## What about aiming high?

When we build from success to success, we are aiming high, but doing it in steps. However, sometimes taking a chance at a big leap forward without doing the groundwork is worthwhile, too, and can be exhilarating.

Even if a goal appears unobtainable right now, it is still worth having the courage to give it a shot. We might be lucky and hit it! So that is part of the process of going beyond our limitations, too.

However, if we do this repeatedly and fail at hitting the goal, we lose ground and have to make it up again by doing additional careful stepwise work.

## "Practicing is making SUCCESS a habit."

Since 1988 there has been a sign in my studio that says "Practicing is making SUCCESS a habit." That concept can be easy to forget, but my students certainly hear it a lot!

# REPEATEDLY DOING SOMETHING WELL
# The Best Use of Your Practice Time

## *Example: Improving Your Intonation*

If you want to improve your intonation on a particular passage, figure out a way that you can play the notes in tune.

Devise a method that will enable you to play each note correctly, and then repeat that until it becomes reliable.

## Suggestions of methods to try:

### 1. Slower

Could you play each note in tune if you played it slowly?

### 2. Stop-Prepare

Can you get it right if you use Stop-Prepare (pause between the notes and then consciously choose where to place your next finger)? It is best to do Stop-Prepare with an intentional rhythm, so use the metronome. Add a one or two beat rest for the time you need to stop and prepare the next note.

### 3. Tuner, open strings

Would it help to use an electronic tuner to find out where those notes are on the fingerboard? Can you check with any open strings to see if the note is right?

## 4. Finger spacings

Note the finger spacings from one note to the next. How close are they to the other fingers? Be sure you know the distance between them. Notice how your fingers feel when they are in the right place on the fingerboard, and how they feel when they are in the right relationship to each other. Memorize that feeling.

## 5. Hear it before playing it

Can you hear what each note should be before you play it? Can you sing the intervals? Playing the passage on the piano first can help you to know what it should sound like. Sing what you think the next note is before playing it on the piano.

## 6. Play with the piano

If you have someone who can play the passage on the piano while you play it on the violin, doing that could help a lot. Having the piano play an octave lower is usually better than in unison. If you have a digital recorder, you can play it on the piano yourself and then play the violin with the recording. Some keyboards will also record it and play it back.

## 7. Make all the notes the same length

Play every note as a quarter note, rather than the rhythm as it occurs in the piece. That way you will be able to focus totally on the finger placements. Play with a solid, healthy, loud tone so you hear it clearly.

## 8. Double stops

If the notes are on two strings, play them as double stops and remember the way your fingers feel in relation to each other as well as your hand position.

**As you are practicing in those ways, remember to:**

- **Enjoy hitting it right on.**

- **Feel the satisfaction** you get from the vibration and resonance the instrument gives you when the note is just right.

- **Repeat until it is easy and solid.**

Once you find a way that you can get the note(s) in tune, do it repeatedly until it feels easy and reliable. Once you can do it easily, play it at least 5-10 more times in a row without mistakes. Memorize that experience and the feeling of security you now have as you play it.

- **Yes!**

Enjoy the feeling of knowing that you can do it now. Have a "Yes!" feeling each time you play it in tune. Like the man who kept hitting the target, your pattern can be:

## Success, Rejoice, Satisfaction.

# Building from Success to Success in LIFE

### Story: One Success Builds to Greater Successes

I once met a man in his mid-twenties who already owned and operated a very successful piano business. He did not even have a college degree, and yet he had a large number of employees, three of whom had PhD's. He had already gained an international reputation in piano sales, and he had made a lot of money, too!

How did this happen?

When Mark was about 14 years old, someone gave him an old upright piano that was in sorry need of some major repairs. He had a wonderful time tinkering with it and learning about how a piano works. Eventually, he got it fixed up and sold it. He was thrilled with his ability to do it and with the profit it brought him!

With the money from the sale of the piano, he bought a do-it-yourself kit with all the pieces needed to build a harpsichord. He built the harpsichord and sold that at a tidy profit as well.

That enabled him to buy another bigger and better kit . . . Within about ten years he owned two warehouses full of Bechstein grand pianos and a lucrative international business.

Mark's success was built by first being successful at a small goal and then building upward and outward from there. Success builds on success.

===

## Story: "I can play every note in every piece of music."

At the time that Mary Elizabeth Leach finished high school and applied to music school, the three top places to study music were the Julliard School, the New England Conservatory of Music, and the Curtis Institute. The chances of being admitted to one of these schools, especially as a pianist, were slim. To say that it was competitive would be an understatement.

Mary Elizabeth chose to apply to the New England Conservatory, and was not only accepted, but was one of the few piano majors to receive a nearly full-tuition scholarship (based on her skills).

Many years later she told me, "The most important breakthrough in my musical development came when I was in the 6th grade. It suddenly occurred to me that I had ten fingers, and I knew how to read and play every single note on the piano, so I could play virtually any piano piece in the world, provided I played it slowly enough!

"I got excited, and asked my father – who was a musician himself – what the most difficult piece of music was that we had in the house. He pulled it off the shelf for me. I was completely confident that I could learn it, and so I did, one note at a time.

"After that, nothing stopped me. I knew that I could play anything."

The piece she learned to play was Mendelssohn's Rondo Capriccioso. In the years to come, it became one of her signature pieces. In fact, it was one of the pieces she played for her audition at the conservatory.

How was she able to play such a difficult piece?

"At first I played each individual note so slowly that it was almost absurd, but even at that pace, I made sure to learn the notes in the correct rhythm. I practiced with a metronome. I went through the piece from beginning to end, over and over. Gradually, I turned up the speed on the metronome. After I became familiar with all of the notes, I practiced the more difficult sections individually."

===

*Building from one success to the next*
*is a sure way to reach your goal*
*and to have a tremendous amount of*
*enjoyment and satisfaction along the way.*

## CHAPTERS in
## *Success with the Violin & Life*

**1. Practice Being Successful**
   Building from Success to Success in Life
**2. Setting Goals**
   Overall Goals in Life
**3. Which Skill Sets Do You Need?**
   Which Skill Sets Do You Need for Life?
**4. How Does It Go?**
   Holding a Clear Vision of What You Intend to Create in Life
**5. Meeting Challenges**
   Meeting Life's Challenges
**6. Effective Strategies – Where, Why, How?**
   Effective Strategies for Achieving Goals in Life

**7. What Are You Practicing**
Forming Habits in Daily Life

**8. Embody the Feeling**
*Embodying the Feeling*: The Most Important Component in Manifesting What You Want in Life

**9. Repetition & Erasing Mistakes**
Mistakes, Apologies & Forgiveness in Life

**10. Upgrading Your Overall Technique**
Improving Life Skills

**11. Vibrato**
Combining Technical Expertise and Passion

**12. Strategies for Solid Memorization**
Effective Memorization in Life

**13. Practice Time – Getting the Most Out of It**
Time Management

**14. Using Circumstances to Our Advantage**
Letting Life Circumstances Bring Us Benefit

**15. Choosing a Teacher**
Choosing Mentors

**16. Playing in Groups**
Finding Your Tribe

**17. Performing at Your Best**
Fear Does Not Need to Stop Us – Handling Emotions

**18. Reviewing & Looking Back**
Updating Our Relationships

**19. Using the Metronome**
The Pulse of Life: Living in Harmony or Dissonance

**20. Entrainment & Sympathetic Vibration**
One Person Can Make a Big Difference

www.ingramcontent.com/pod-product-compliance
Lightning Source LLC
Chambersburg PA
CBHW070551010526
44118CB00012B/1290